BRISTOL 403

JOHN MANLEY

AMBERLEY

*For my wife, Sandra, whose constant support has been essential to
the production of this book*

First published 2024

Amberley Publishing
The Hill, Stroud,
Gloucestershire, GL5 4EP

www.amberley-books.com

ISBN: 978 1 3981 1670 2 (print)
ISBN: 978 1 3981 1671 9 (ebook)

British Library Cataloguing in Publication Data.
A catalogue record for this book is available from the British Library.

Typeset in 10pt on 13pt Celeste.
Typesetting by SJmagic DESIGN SERVICES, India.
Printed in the UK.

Contents

Foreword
by Sir George S. J. White

Within weeks of the end of the First World War, the government cancelled the majority of orders for military aircraft. My grandfather Sir G. Stanley White, who was joint founder and managing director of the British & Colonial Aeroplane Company (later known as the Bristol Aeroplane Company), found himself with some 4,000 employees and almost no orders for his company's products. It was the beginning of years of struggle to keep his workforce employed and to maintain their unique skills.

War broke out again in 1938 and by 1941, the prospect of victory seemed bleak. Even so, remembering the years of industrial hardship following the 1918 Armistice, Sir Stanley instructed my father (his son) George. S. M. White to draw up plans for what alternative products the Aircraft Company might make when and indeed if peace returned. By this time his employees numbered some 60,000, so a repeat of his earlier experience was unthinkable. Among other carefully set out suggestions that my father made was the manufacture of a six-cylinder car, which would enjoy 'high speed performance coupled with silence and comfort'; in other words a 'small Bentley'. Quality and customer care were to be of paramount importance.

My father's paper predicted that there would be a high demand for new cars if victory was achieved and highlighted the importance of taking advantage of this opportunity. At the same time, he noted that while the war lasted, the Bristol Aeroplane Company would be in no position to indulge in car design and development. He suggested therefore that an existing company, such as ERA or Aston Martin, should be taken over when the war ended and that an upgraded version of their pre-war products should be rapidly designed, built and marketed, to give time for Bristol to develop a model of its own.

This, as John Manley explains so lucidly, is exactly what happened. Within weeks of the end of the war in Europe, the Bristol Aeroplane Company bought a controlling share in AFN, the pre-war manufacturer of Frazer Nash cars, which had obtained the rights to import and assemble BMWs in Britain before hostilities broke out. The first Bristol, the 400, was effectively an upgraded amalgam of BMW design, produced at lightning speed and launched onto a very appreciative public. Meanwhile the 401, the first of the three models which are the subject of this book, was being developed in the background.

It would be perfectly reasonable to claim therefore that the 401, designed and developed under my father's direction (as all Bristol Cars were until 1973), was the first true Bristol car.

Gathering clouds in the aircraft division in the later 1950s meant that the Bristol Aeroplane Company had to reduce investment in its car division, just at a time when important innovation was taking place there. This was followed by forced mergers by the government of all independent British aircraft manufacturers, which stripped Bristol Cars of its vast parent company and substantial financial backing. The period of the six-cylinder Bristol-engined Bristol car, stretching from 1945 to 1960, might reasonably be described as the Golden Age of the marque.

It is hard to believe that after the publication of this book, there will not be a stampede to buy all remaining Bristol cars of this period. John Manley not only describes their virtues in a way that will fascinate the non-technical reader but does so in a way that will certainly capture the attention of the expert. He describes the ethos behind their design and manufacture with unusual understanding. His book is written with the same care, sensitivity and artistry that was lavished on the cars themselves. It is a pleasure to read and will, I am certain, be a pleasure to own.

Author's Foreword

I shall always blame Robin Pitman for inspiring my interest in Bristol cars. He was my revered art master at school, an artist in his own right, who suddenly one day in 1953 turned up at the school with a brand-new Bristol 403 car. This sensational vehicle, which was regarded as a supercar at that time, sat well adjacent to the seventeenth-century

A display of cars on the Brabazon runway at Filton, including examples of the aerodynes and other later models. (Mark Bishop)

An array of cars built by Bristol Aeroplane Company Car Division, including the 450 Le Mans racing car on the extreme left of the photograph. (Bristol Owners Heritage Trust (BOHT))

cloisters of Sir William Borlase's school at Marlow, in leafy Buckinghamshire. The arrival of the car was soon followed by Mr Pitman giving a design tutorial to twenty young boys on the virtues of the new Bristol 403.

An hour of design analysis commenced with the statement that 'this example of automobile design is, and always will be, a design icon'. The term stayed with me thereafter and influenced my decision many years later. It is a description which I have heard frequently from several quarters and the purpose of this book is to justify such an accolade. Many of us boys came away with a dream of owning a Bristol 403 one day in the future. It took me until 1972 to realise this dream. Since the Bristol came into our lives, it has been, and continues to be, a cherished mode of transport in the Manley household. Although I had always kept an eye on the Bristol car models as they developed, since my early introduction to the Bristol 403, I came across by chance, a private advert in our local paper, the *Bristol Evening Post*. This was advertising for sale a 1953 Bristol 403, the same model that the art master had brought into school nineteen years previously. By that time, cars of that age were considered just old cars and did not have the classic status that they have today. The princely sum of £325 changed hands to allow me to become the proud owner of the Bristol. It was completely roadworthy and therefore I could drive it home with a smile per mile, feeling like Toad of Toad Hall from the children's storybook *Wind in the Willows*.

An immaculate late example of a 403 dating from 1955. (Andrew Gibbs)

My elation was a little marred by the reception from my work colleagues that my new mode of transport received. I had previously owned a new Lotus Europa sports car that I had built from a kit to save purchase tax. My contemporaries could not comprehend why I had sold such a vehicle to acquire what they described as 'an old man's car'. The contrast was rather dramatic, and it is not surprising that the purity of the engineering and the esoteric design was difficult to appreciate compared to the modern Lotus. This may have been because the Lotus Europa, based on the design of the Lotus type 47, was basically a racing car designed for road use and this particularly appealed to young men. Although the Lotus derived from a racing heritage and was certainly quick, it had drawbacks when used as a road car. The very low seating position meant that on roads with undulations it was difficult to see approaching vehicles which could be hidden in a dip in the road and suddenly appear when overtaking slower traffic. Another surprising characteristic of the Lotus was a tendency in wet conditions to continue straight on rather than turn when entering a bend. This was alleviated to some extent by placing a bag of cement in the front luggage compartment, which gave more adhesion in such conditions. No doubt suitable racing tyres may have made all the difference as handling in dry conditions was excellent. The fine handling of the 403 in wet or dry conditions was a welcome relief and the higher seating position made for a generally safer and a more relaxed driving experience.

Despite disparaging comments from my colleagues, the Bristol soon became our only means of transport and gave us many years of reliable motoring at home and abroad until

Lotus Europa based on a type 47 Lotus racing car. (Author)

our fourth child arrived. It was not possible to fit four children and two adults in the car with modern child safety protection, so the inevitable Volvo estate, with additional rear facing seats, came into the household. This situation led to a degree of neglect in relation to the Bristol. It languished in the garden of our property until we acquired a house with a double garage. During this period the adage of 'use it or lose it' came to mind as the neglect did give cause for concern as to whether we should keep the Bristol. Fortunately, we decided to retain the car and make plans for a restoration programme. Mark Bishop, a friend who had been inspired to buy a 403 after seeing mine, had restored a similar model some years previously. It was a cause for celebration when I managed to bring my car back to its former glory and we were able to display the cars side by side at a meeting of classic cars in Queen Square in Bristol. The restoration took some time but was eventually achieved three weeks before the Annual Bristol Owners' Club Concours[2] held at Greenwich Naval College in 2011. The trip from Bristol to Greenwich in mid-summer, with a new tight engine and London traffic congestion, made the car run somewhat warm, which caused a few nasty moments. When we eventually arrived, with time to carry out last minute titivation before the judging took place, the trials of the journey were soon forgotten by the car's public reception. Other car enthusiasts and the public at large, most of whom were there to see the Greenwich Naval College and not cars, were overwhelmed with enthusiasm. The judges were similarly impressed, and we were delighted to receive first prize in the Anthony Crook class, which judged vehicles in the 401-403 category. We did not know at the time that our car was in fact the first 403 off the production line, probably the show car at Earl's Court Motor Show in 1953 and was also featured in the original sales brochure, so it was rather fitting that it received this accolade.

Above: The author's dark blue 403 contrasted with a maroon 403 owned by Mark Bishop against the backdrop of Queen Square, Bristol. (Mark Bishop)

Below: The author's 403 at the Bristol Owner's Club Concourse in Greenwich in 2011. (Author)

Concourse prize winners at Greenwich in 2011. (Mark Bishop)

Extract from a sales brochure – an image of a Bristol 403. (BOHT)

Acknowledgements

I am grateful to Sir George White Bart for agreeing to provide a foreword to this book and for the many conversations I have had with him that have added to my knowledge of the Bristol marque. My thanks are also due to Bristol Owners' Heritage Trust[1] and in particular to Stefan Cembrowicz, Chair of the Trust, for giving me access to the Bristol archives, providing many photos, reading my drafts and being a mine of information. Generous assistance has been given by many other people such as Michael Palmer, Geoff Kingston, Andrew Gibbs, Paul Hickman, Sebastian Gross and others who have allowed me to use their photographic images. Finally, many thanks to Mark Bishop, a fellow 403 owner, for years of assistance in restoring my own Bristol 403, for critically evaluating the manuscript, for providing photographs and for making useful suggestions of matters that should be included.

Every attempt has been made to seek permission for copyright material used in this book. However, if we have inadvertently used copyright material without permission or acknowledgement, we apologise and will make the necessary adjustment at the first opportunity.

Introduction

According to L. J. K Setright,[3] the term aerodyne was devised from Greek roots to describe a body shaped to move efficiently through the air and be acted on favourably by air. It was devised apparently by a scholar called Dr Frederick Lanchester, who was studying aerodynamics. The streamlined aerodynamically efficient lines of the three models that are the subjects of this book, aptly suit Lanchester's definition. They include the 401, 402 and 403 and they are collectively known as the aerodynes. These models, with their avant-garde styling and a design, that is post-war rather than pre-war in spirit, marked a turning point in car design. Chapter two explains how the design process evolved and how the aerodyne styling emerged from a sophisticated design process that drew heavily on the experience of designing and building aircraft. The emergence of the 403 as a culmination of this process is described in chapter three. Chapter four gives a more detailed description of how the car was made, effectively by hand, using the skills of engineers who had been used to innovating and developing ideas rapidly during the Second World War. In chapter five the focus is on the attention paid to detailed aspects of the design that are so intrinsic to the success of the aerodyne cars. The way in which specialised coach builders in the UK and Europe responded enthusiastically to the opportunity that the rolling chassis of the Bristol 400 and 401 provided is explained in chapter six. The chassis could be used as a basis for their own interpretations of a quality car. The consequence was a range of different body shapes, some of which were successful, but others less so. Chapter seven describes public and professional reactions to the car designs in the past and today. The introduction of the 401 caused a sensation when launched at the 1948 Earl's Court Motor Show. Oxley summed this up in 1988 by stating here was 'a car of the future, not the past!'.

It could be argued that the Bristol Aeroplane Company, in producing the three models of the aerodyne family, achieved a design that has rarely been surpassed and the 403, with its final refinements, could indeed be described as a design icon. Chapter eight justifies this claim and explains why the car deserves the label iconic. In the conclusion the reason why so many people describe the car shape as perfect or beautiful are explored by reference to the Golden Section, a principle that has influenced designers, either knowingly or unwittingly, since ancient times. A postscript explains the rather sad story of what has happened to the Bristol Car Company in recent years. The three aerodyne models that are relevant to this book are described below, although to tell the story, it is necessary to explain how the first post-war car made by the company came about, so the development of the 400, the predecessor of the aerodynes, is also explained.

Bristol 401
introduced at
1948 Earl's Court
Motor Show.
(BOHT)

Bristol 401

Introduced in 1948 at the Geneva Motor Show, this four- to five-seater sports saloon had a maximum speed of 97 mph and achieved 0–60mph in 17.4 seconds. The engine is a type 85C six-cylinder inline configuration with an aluminium head and cast-iron block construction. Engine capacity is 1,971cc. The carburettors were three 32B1 Solex. It achieved 85 bhp (brake horsepower) at 4,500 revs. The maximum speed is 97 mph.

Bristol 402

Nicknamed the Hollywood Special when it was introduced in 1948 at the Earl's Court Motor Show, the 402 is a four-seater drophead convertible. It has the same engine configuration as the 401.

The Hollywood Special, the 402 drophead convertible in the foreground displayed at Greenwich. (Mark Bishop)

Bristol 403

The 403 was introduced in May 1953. It was modified considerably by the installation of a new engine, the type 100A, but its external appearance remained almost unchanged. The re-designed engine produced 100 bhp at 5,000 revs. The maximum speed is 104 mph with 0–60 mph in approximately 13 seconds.

A Bristol 403 at Filton with a Bristol Aeroplane Company helicopter flying just above it. (BOHT)

1

Emergence of the Bristol Car Division

During both world wars Bristol Aeroplane Company was crucial to the war effort. The company, founded in 1910 by the great-grandfather of the current Sir George White, had vast experience of aeroplane design even before the Second World War broke out in 1939. It was already a significant aeroplane manufacturer in the world context. During the war they expanded their premises and massively increased their output. At least 70,000 people were employed. The flurry of aircraft building meant that the company developed the expertise in design and methods of production and were soon nationally known for the outstanding fighter bombers such as the Blenheim and Beaufighter that were essential contributors to the war effort. The workforce was extremely skilled in both design and production and able to work to very short time scales. The period after the Second World War from 1945 commenced with a slump in the British economy, which to some extent was reflected internationally. This situation resulted in a thirteen per cent drop in the UK Gross Domestic Product (GDP) during 1947, which affected

A fighter bomber, the Bristol Blenheim developed by Bristol Aeroplane Company. (BOHT)

Above: A Bristol Beaufighter. (BOHT)

Right: The front cover of the Festival of Britain programme of 1951. (Ian H. Cox, HMSO)

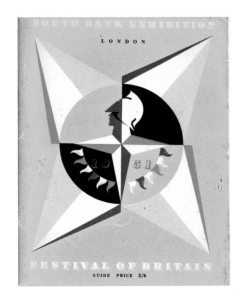

the whole of the British economy. This period of adversity, marked by continued rationing, left the public with a thirst for change and new products. This thirst for change was fuelled by the Festival of Britain in 1951, which promoted British products. The succession of a new young queen in 1952 added to this desire for change and new products to reflect the new Elizabethan era. The spread of a more modern style reflected the growth of modernist ideas across Europe and the USA that was permeating every field of activity. The shortage of all types of manufactured products during the war led to a pent-up demand as manufacturing was concentrated on goods required for the war effort. Luxury goods had not been available for the more affluent members of society, so manufacturers turned their attention to satisfying this demand.

Pent-up demand was no more apparent than in the motor car market, where the emphasis on the war effort had curtailed the development of new models. The Bristol Aeroplane Company, in its former guise as the British and Colonial Aeroplane Company, had previously faced the issue of attempting to retain their skilled workforce after the First World War (1914–18). The same problem emerged after the Second World War Two (1939–45). At that time diversification led the company into another area of industry in the form of sailing dinghies, helicopters, invalid cars, prefabricated buildings, buses, and commercial vehicles bodies. Many of these fine machines are still in operation. Again, there was a desire to retain skilled staff who had worked in the aircraft industry in the hope that the market for passenger aircraft would burgeon as the economy revived. It was in this climate that the Bristol Aeroplane Company considered diversification into other areas of manufacturing, including the production of a high-quality luxury sports saloon. This led to the formation of the Car Division of the Bristol Aeroplane Company. The inspiration for setting up the Car Division was Sir George S. M. White, father of the current Sir George White, who had been working on the idea of setting up a car division since 1941. Sir George continued to lead the company from this date until his retirement on health grounds in 1973. It is certain that Sir George was the driving force. His philosophy and ethical standards led the way towards creating cars of great quality and he personally inspired great loyalty in the workforce. It is not totally surprising that the Car Division's search for a suitable basis for their post-war models should focus on the German engineered BMW design. The BMW series, introduced at the 1936 Berlin Motor Show, was successful in pre-war competitions and was regarded highly as an innovative machine.

The first model produced by Bristol Aeroplane Company was the Bristol 400. Work commenced on a number of protypes in 1946 using a combination of the chassis components

A gathering of Bristol cars and buses at Kemble airfield in 2022 in honour of the Bristol Britannia aircraft, otherwise known as the Whispering Giant. (Adrian@photoairpress.plus.com)

Right: A Bristol bus in running order currently in use for weddings and other events. (Author)

Below: An early example of a Bristol 400 at Filton. (BOHT)

of the BMW 326 with the BMW 328 engine. The development of the 400 was assisted because of the contacts and cooperation which had been ongoing between AFN Frazer Nash and the Bristol Car Division. AFN stood for the initials of the founder of the Frazer Nash company, Archibald Frazer-Nash. It was set up in 1922 and was already a well-known and respected British sports car producer before the Second World War. The company had a pre-war licence to produce BMWs and after the war they were instrumental in assisting the Car Division in their negotiations with BMW, as AFN had been the British importer of BMW cars since 1934. Before the Second World War, it had already been agreed that AFN Frazer Nash would assemble the BMW models under licence in the UK. The outbreak of hostilities, plus the opinion that the potential purchasers might have some degree of resistance towards products associated with a former adversary, led to the collapse of the market. In late 1945, cooperation between Bristol Car Division and AFN reached a stage where a delegation from both companies travelled together to the BMW factory in Munich to obtain drawings for the BMW 326, 327 and 328 models. The drawings, of course, were all in metric and had to be converted to imperial before production in the factory could take place.

AFN Frazer Nash continued to produce their sports cars utilising the new Bristol 2-litre engine developed from the pre-war BMW unit. AFN had the licence to build but did not have all the facilities of production to build a complete motor car, hence the need for co-operation. The arrangement was mutually beneficial in the post-war context and continued until 1947. Engines and components were supplied by the Car Division to AFN who continued to build their own version of sports cars until 1955. The 400 was unveiled at the 1948 Geneva Motor Show. It is not surprising, given the common heritage, that the BMW 327 and the Bristol 400 have some similarities. Indeed, these two models and the

Bristol 400 and a BMW 327 showing the resemblance between the two models. (Michael Palmer)

From left to right, Bristol 400 drophead, BMW 327 and Bristol 400 showing the family resemblance between these models. (Michael Palmer)

AFN variants are often confused. The distinctive oval radiator grills, for example, are a common characteristic that often makes it difficult for people who are trying to identify the make of car.

The testing of vehicles through competition is the ultimate research and development model with performance, reliability and longevity being displayed in arduous conditions on the track or in rallies which tests components to the full. Although the pre-war BMW cars were generally revered and were very successful in competition, the quality of the chassis and some aspects of the engine fell well below what the Car Division were contemplating for their new luxury sports saloons. For this reason, the chassis was re-engineered, and the engine specification was upgraded using aircraft quality materials. The final version of the Bristol 400 model received numerous accolades from customers and the motoring press. The quality of the cars was never in doubt coming from the manufacturers of some of the world's most renowned aircraft. Many motoring journalists recognised these aspects of the vehicles during their extensive road tests. In 9 January 1948 edition, the respected car magazine *Autocar* waxed lyrical in a road test and commented: 'The buyer obtains a connoisseur's car, attractive to look upon, comfortable to ride in and a constant delight to

Fraser Nash sports car showing the common characteristics of these cars based on BMW designs. (Geoff Kingston)

The oval design of the radiator grilles is a common characteristic. (Norman Shirlaw)

handle because of the accuracy of control and responsiveness of the performance.' Palmer reinforced this opinion more recently in 2015 in a similar vein: 'Bristol had managed to create a discreet and well-engineered vehicle, with performance and handling to match, in a remarkably short time.'

Exclusivity and excellence became the hallmark for the Car Division's products. Production rates remained low, but can be attributed, at least in part, to Bristol Cars determination to achieve high quality and the use of labour-intensive coachbuilding methods, many aspects of which were finished by hand. This made the cars very expensive, which must have deterred some buyers. Although developed in such a short space of time, the Bristol 400 became one of the most successful models with a production run of 667 cars and many sporting achievements. The combination of a compact body and lightweight construction was effective. The bonnet and doors were panelled in aluminium and a sophisticated suspension system was devised. The revised BMW engine resulted in what became the renowned 2-litre six-cylinder engine. In consequence, the Bristol 400 became a successful competitor in many spheres of motorsport. It achieved first place in 1948 Polish rally, first of the British entries in the Monte Carlo Rally and third place overall in 1949.

Sporting successes of the Bristol 400. (BOHT)

With in-house design expertise and familiarity with materials, particularly aluminium and the other unique resources available to them, it is not altogether surprising that the Car Division of the Bristol Aeroplane Company was able to produce such a remarkable sports saloon in their first foray into this competitive area of automobile manufacture. Many established car makers were producing their post-war production models to meet the burgeoning market, so competition was fierce. Cars such as Riley, Sunbeam, MG and many more came to the market with new designs, but none approaching the quality, refinement and cost of the Bristol model. It was on this foundation of the success of their first attempt at car design that the company turned its attention to the next model, where their aircraft design and production skills could be developed to the full.

A Bristol 400 on the runway at Filton alongside an aircraft. (Stefan Cembrowicz)

2

The Evolving Design – the Aerodynes

A good run in a classic car, such as a Bristol, can be according to Balfour in 2019 'like traversing the earth on winged feet'. It is not surprising therefore that the Car Division used the winged horse, Pegasus, as a badge on their coachwork for the aerodyne models when they were introduced. It is worth speculating on how the development of the 400, which was essentially a pre-Second World War design, turned into the 401, which according to L. J. K. Setright has the distinction of 'being one of the most outstanding body designs to ever appear'. During these early stages of the production of the first 400 model, research was already taking place to produce a more aerodynamic sports saloon. The design process embarked on is instructive because it demonstrates a research-based approach to finding a solution that would meet their aims to produce an outstanding vehicle. The diagram below illustrates the process.

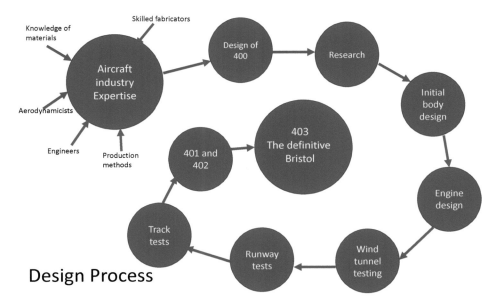

Design Process

The stages in the development of the 401 and aerodynes. (Author)

Above and below: Touring designed car which formed the basis of the 401 design. (BOHT with the assistance of Michael Palmer)

BRISTOL SUPERLEGGERA

A Touring designed car that influenced the design of the 401, but was regarded by the Car Division as rather bulbous and lumpen. (BOHT with the assistance of Michael Palmer)

Two women demonstrating the lightness of the superleggera frame of an unknown Italian make.

There is no doubt that the 400 had a more luxurious and more pleasing design than some of the earlier models and its sporting achievements were impressive. It is a design that remains very popular to this day. However, successful as it was in terms of sales and sporting achievements, in some quarters it was felt that there was a need for a more spacious and luxurious model to reach the emerging sophisticated market. Furthermore, the design was felt to be evocative of the pre-war period. To this end the search began for a more stylish design solution which would counter criticism of the 400 model as having undertones of a pre-war design concept rather than a more modern image. This search led to the renowned Italian automobile and coachwork design specialists of the time in Milan and Turin. They were known for their production of cars with considerable design flair. Bristol Car Division directors visited the factories of Carrozzeria Touring of Milan and Pinin Farina SA of Turin where they were impressed with the styling of models being produced. The next step was for the Car Division to investigate further the potential for cooperation with Touring to produce a new model. Dudley Hobbs, chief designer at the Car Division, visited Milan to inspect examples of their products and was said to be impressed by the lines of the Touring-built superleggera Lancia Aprilia bodies. Superleggera is Italian for lightweight, as illustrated by the photo showing two Italian women holding the framework of an unknown vehicle. It was not just the innovative styling and the comprehensive use of aluminium for the coachwork, which was attractive to the Bristol contingent, but also the lightweight structure used by the Italians, which supported the body panels. It consisted of a series of small diameter steel tubes welded together to form a framework for the aluminium body panels. The result was a very strong, but extremely lightweight construction that was well suited to the firm's manufacturing techniques. Although Hobbs gave a favourable report on the overall design of the Lancia, he had reservations regarding the quality of workmanship. According to Balfour in 2009, director Verdon-Smith also felt that the quality of the workmanship, particularly as regards welding standards, was lacking and stated, 'for some of the welded joints I think I would do at least as well myself'. However, he did concede that 'we do need

An operative at Filton welding parts of the chassis. The framework is clearly visible. (BOHT)

the flair for artistic achievement which they possess'. To achieve this Touring brought two cars to Bristol, one complete and one partially completed, to be used to coach Filton staff on the superleggera form of construction and to develop the design concept. Carlo Anderloni, a key member of the Touring company staff from Milan, remained for three months to assist in the development process of applying this system to a Bristol chassis.

Using the lightweight construction method would result in a much lighter vehicle for its size than would be possible with traditional steel and timber construction. This would improve power to weight ratios, an advantage to a manufacturer intent on producing a high-quality, high-performance vehicle. The final body shape evolved from a complex and interactive process which tended to allow numerous members of the workforce to have an input in the evolution of the final shape. The opportunity for many employees to be involved in the design process was a clever and innovative idea on the part of the directors, as it gave the operatives a sense of ownership of the design, a belief in its authenticity and a desire to achieve an outstanding vehicle. The final shape was achieved with the building of a timber formwork, normally referred to as a buck or horse. The original bucks have recently come into the ownership of the Bristol Owners' Heritage Trust. The joinery used in preparing these bucks is notable, as it is of outstanding quality. Several of the bucks are now displayed in motor museums throughout the country. Using the bucks to enable the three-dimensional form to be seen and assessed for suitability became an essential part of the process of production. In developing the ideal shape, the company were not completely satisfied with the resultant form based on the Italian prototype. The next stage was the use of inordinate amounts of flexible plasticine filler to modify the original Touring design by eye and aluminium panels were then shaped to the form of the buck. Once the design was felt to be acceptable the modified buck was then used to craft a true to scale model for wind tunnel testing for aerodynamic efficiency. To this end the company were aided by having access to aerodynamicists and wind tunnel facilities that were used in aircraft design. The scale models of the design were tested in the wind tunnel and adapted as necessary.

Once the basic shape was acceptable the design process was not over. The lengths to which the Car Division went in their quest for a perfect product was demonstrated by their

The front end of the timber buck to act as the formwork for a 401. (Stefan Cembrowicz)

An alternative view of the timber buck showing form of construction. (Stefan Cembrowicz)

Aluminium being shaped by operatives. The framework is clearly visible. (BOHT)

Right: An operative working on the shaping of the aluminium to the superleggera frame to form the edge of the roof. (BOHT)

Below left: A tenth scale model in the wind tunnel. (BOHT)

Below right: Aerodynamicist checking results of wind tunnel testing. (BOHT)

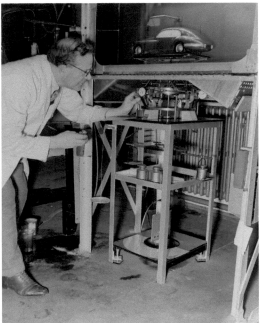

approach to the aerodynamic efficiency of the new body shape. Not satisfied that wind tunnel testing alone was sufficient to determine aerodynamic efficiency, they embarked on a process of testing a full-size model. The 2-mile-long runway at Filton, originally extended to facilitate the giant Brabazon aircraft taking off, was a facility that few car manufacturers had available. It meant that data from the wind tunnel tests could be validated and supplemented by driving full-size vehicles at high speed on the runway. Wool tufts were attached to the body at crucial points to demonstrate airflow This was filmed enabling the engineers to fine tune adjustments to create the greatest possible aerodynamic efficiency. In addition, it facilitated a study of the way in which exhaust fumes behaved at different speeds. This was done by mixing oil into the petrol to blacken the exhaust fumes so that the resultant pattern of exhaust gases could be analysed. The result of this research was that the engineers repositioned the exhaust tailpipe to exit at the side of the car rather than at the rear. This was to ensure that exhaust gases would not enter the interior of the car. Research to investigate the angle of roll and effect of side winds on the vehicle when driven at speed or when cornering was also undertaken.

The body shape that resulted from this research was, even by modern standards, aerodynamically successful. L. J. K. Setright, when writing in 1974, felt that the aerodynamic characteristics of the aerodynes as measured by drag coefficient achieved 'not only by the standards of the time, but also a generation later, aerodynamically one of the best and most efficient production cars in the world.' The success of wind tunnel testing by the company resulted in many famous manufacturers requesting tests of their own new models at the facility in Filton, Bristol. Rumour has it that the testing found that some new models from renowned car manufacturers were likely to go up to 15 mph faster if they went backwards rather than forwards. If this is true it must have been rather embarrassing for the designers concerned.

High-speed testing of 401s on the Brabazon Runway at Filton. (BOHT)

Testing the aerodynamic efficiency of the car's form by observing airflow through a series of tufts attached to the body. (BOHT)

The evolution of the aerodyne models, Bristol 401, 402 and 403, although heavily influenced by the Touring connection, developed through the combined efforts of Sir George White and Dudley Hobbs who were determined that the new model would fully embrace the ideology of the Bristol company; an ideology that was based on sound engineering and robust quality. The aim was to produce a vehicle which not only had unusually high aerodynamic qualities, but was also built to a standard that would give a durable and refined product for the discerning purchasers of these luxury cars. One notable characteristic of the company was that the design process never totally ended as ongoing refinements were constantly produced. For example, the early examples of the 401 had a ridge along the bottom edge of the body between the wheel arches and an air vent in the front wing on either side of the bonnet. Both these features tended to detract from the smoothness and aesthetic qualities of the car, but the ridges were removed on later models. The lower body ridge was retained on the convertibles until production ceased in 1950. The characteristics of the final design of the 403 resulted in a smooth exterior with minimal obstruction to airflow. The push button doors of the vehicle are a significant characteristic of the design. This solution ensures that there is no interruption of airflow that would result from projecting door handles.

The new aerodyne model 401 had a superior performance to the similarly powered 400 The 401 was substantially larger than the earlier model, as there was an increase in volume of the 401 body and it was also 55 kilograms heavier than the 400, but performance was nevertheless considerably enhanced by the streamlining. The 401 model had a top speed, as tested by *Autosport* in 1952, of approximately 97 mph compared to the 400 model's top speed of 90-plus mph and the 401 also reduced the 0–60 mph time by almost two seconds. Recommended cruising speed was 78 mph or 3,570 rpm.

Ridge on the bottom of the body shell of an early 401. An air vent is visible on the side of the front wings. Both these features were later removed. (BOHT)

The ridge along the bottom of the 402 illustrated is clearly visible. (Geoff Kingston)

The push button door opening is flush with the bodywork. The design avoids any obstruction to airflow that may have reduced aerodynamic efficiency if included. (Mark Bishop)

The second aerodyne model to be produced was the 402, which was a convertible body, occasional four-seater open tourer. The initial examples were built by Carrozzeria Pinin Farina SA, of Turin, but these were very much decried by the Bristol craftsmen, who felt that the excessive amount of filler used by the Italian makers in the custom-built body was unacceptable. This was compounded when the cloth upholstery of the imported models was found to be infested with maggots. The cars were hastily moved outside the premises and fumigated before being reupholstered in leather. The final modification to the design of the Bristol 402, according to Setright, was to take a hacksaw to the body of a Bristol 401 and take the top off to produce the design solution for future 402 models. This approach seemed to lack the finesse of the much more reasoned approach to the design of the 401 body, but surprisingly the effect was more pleasing than the Italian examples. The 402 was a model which was very much aimed at the American market and had certain decorative features, such as more chrome trim, dashboard in the same colour as the exterior paintwork and ivory coloured control knobs in the cockpit. These features were intended to appeal to customers who might require a more flamboyant appearance than was on offer with the standard aerodyne design of the 401 and later 403 models. A real feather in the cap for the Bristol sales team of the 402 convertibles must have been the sale of two of the cars to the film stars Jean Simmons and Stewart Granger in 1949. Simmons and Granger, a husband-and-wife couple, were then well known through their film careers and were celebrities in both the UK and the USA. Other well-known actresses of the day, such as Yolande Donlan, who appeared in Expresso Bongo alongside Cliff Richard, were used in publicity photographs. This gave rise to the description the 'Hollywood Specials' for the 402s generally, although sales to the American market were rather disappointing. Regardless of this fillip to publicity twenty 402s were built. Some of this sales resistance may have been generated by the complex instructions regarding the raising and stowage of the hood. It was rather intricate and somewhat ingenious, but the factory sales literature did little to encourage confidence in these operations. Besides having detachable cant-rails for the top of the windows, for use when the hood was to be up for extended periods, the hood could be stowed neatly behind the rear seats when not in use. However, the recommendations from the factory warned, 'it cannot be too strongly emphasised that the first steps must be the release of all five press buttons on either side, since to lower

Above: Ivory control knobs were provided on the Hollywood special. (Geoff Kingston)

Left: The actress Yolande Donlan visiting the company for a publicity shot. (BOHT)

the hood with these in situ would result in serious damage'. There were also complaints regarding a degree of scuttle shake, which is often a problem with convertible versions of a saloon model, but not really to be expected of a Bristol car. It is difficult to understand why the 402 convertibles were not more successful than the sales of only twenty models that were built would indicate. Although these criticisms were directed at the 402s, many motoring journalists and owners found them to be very satisfactory and to this day they appear quite stylish. *Classic Automobiles Worldwide* described the model as 'handsome and modern with more than a hint of high-speed capability'. Other accolades came from *Autocar* in November 1948, which referred to the car as a 'workmanlike machine' and felt that it should appeal to the driver who wanted a 'real sports car possessing many of the characteristics of a racing machine, but the tractability to be used on shopping and normal runs'. The short production run of the 402s meant that they never received the improvements that 401s acquired during their development and later the even more significant improvements carried out with introduction of the 403 aerodyne This meant that the 402 still retained the early 401 ridges along the lower body and the prototype still had the air vents in the front side panels, which were not carried forward into production of the later 401 and 403 models. Perhaps the reason for the lack of sales success of the convertible aerodynes may relate to the success of the 401 models.

Demand for the 401 aerodyne models was running at over 128 cars per annum with, according to the factory despatch notes, 514 cars being built during the four-year production run of the 401s from November 1949 to November 1953. The 402 aerodynes, however, were only at the rate of approximately ten cars per year from February 1949 until February 1950 when twenty 402 cars, as verified by copies of despatch notes, were produced. A small car company such as Bristol Cars had limited production capacity and they never adopted mass car production and concentrated on small numbers of quality select vehicles. This buoyant demand for their 401 saloons may have concentrated resources on the production of the 401, as against the 402 convertible models; possibly because the latter appeared to be slow to take off in the export markets for which they were intended.

A blue 400, the first 400 to be built, flanked by a dark red 402 and a mid-blue 401. Photographed on the Brabazon runway at Filton in 2004. (Mark Bishop)

3

The Emergence of the 403

The emergence of the 403 was a result of adaptation and improvement of the 401. The 85A engine used for the 401 had proved to be a reliable unit, but the potential for further development was recognised. Performance was dramatically improved by the development

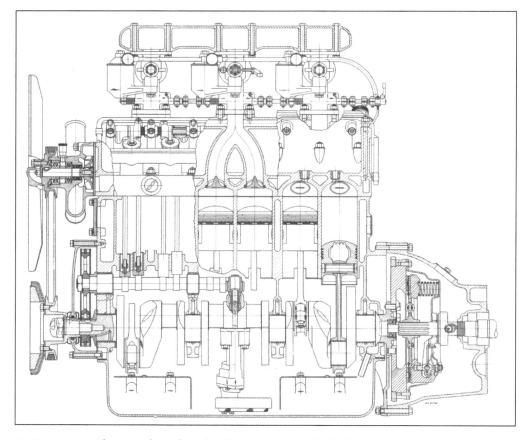

An 85A engine showing downdraught SU carburettors. (BOHT)

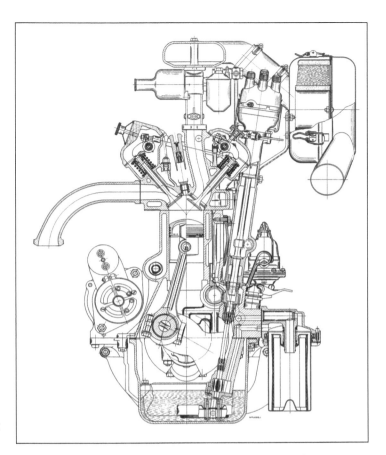

An 85A engine with two-blade fan and rubber crank damper. (BOHT)

of the Bristol 85 type engine into the 100a engine. The design had benefitted from racing experience. It gave an increase from 85 bhp (brake horsepower) at 4,500 revs (revolutions per minute) of the earlier engine to the 100 bhp at 5,000 revs. This was an increase of over 17 per cent, which was achieved by providing larger valves in the cylinder head and lightening the rocker gear to improve the rev range. It took the top speed up to 104 mph with the 0–60 mph time being reduced by four seconds over the 401. Several of the last batch of the 403 models had their compression ratio raised to 8.5 over the previous 7.5, which could give another 5 bhp. To cope with this extra power the sump capacity of the engine was increased to 6.8 litres from its original 4.8 litres and the Hoburn Eaton oil pump was upgraded to give a 50 per cent increase in oil flow for the same revs as on the 85 type engine. The braking system of the 403 was also improved on that of the 401, by installing new aluminium-finned light alloy brake drums with bonded alloy cast-iron liners. Both front and rear drums are finned for better cooling. In addition, a change to the brake pedal leverage reduced the effort required when breaking hard in this more powerful model. There had been criticisms of the amount of pressure that the driver needed to exert for effective braking for both the 401 and 402; hence the modification to the 403.

Other improvements which made the 403 model more desirable, besides increased power of the engine, was the addition of a front torsion anti-roll bar, which improved

Left: An operative examining a 100A cylinder head. (BOHT)

Below: An example of a late 100A engine of a 403 with 8.5 to 1 compression ratio. (Andrew Gibbs)

handling by making the suspension stiffer and reducing roll. The interior heating system was improved to permit adequate demisting of the windscreen and rear window by the addition of subtle vents under the dashboard to direct warm air to where it was required. This worked well when the rear quarter light was open to allow a full throughflow of air, which was aided by a rheostat-controlled fan switch. The rheostat was rather sophisticated in that it initially came on at full power to get an instant response and direct warm air to the interior. It was adjustable and could be turned down if necessary to allow the driver to control air flow and to facilitate directing air flow between the windscreen and the remainder of the car. Improvements in the convenient use of the car were aided by the installation of a modified venting system for the fuel tank, which allowed for full pressure filling of the 77-litre petrol tank without splashback. Externally there were no major alterations to the appearance other than the use of red medallions on the hubcaps, bonnet, and boot together with silver-enamelled front grilles and discreet 403 flashes on either side of the bonnet edges close to the scuttle and on the boot lid.

The principle of continuous development and improvement that was a driving force of the company's philosophy meant that later cars received further modifications. For example,

Above left: Red medallions from a 403. (Timothy Manley)

Above right: Silver grille from a 403. (Mark Bishop)

Below: Art-deco-style chrome 403 bonnet flashes. (Author)

Restrained decorative elements on a 403. (Mark Bishop)

a number of cars were fitted with an overdrive, which made the car quieter at high speeds, improved fuel consumption and resulted in a higher cruising speed for the same engine revs. This was useful for long distance cruising and ultimately was particularly helpful to drivers on the motorway network that commenced with the opening of the M1 motorway in 1959. A further upgrade was the fitting of front disc brakes with servo assistance, which enhanced braking still further. The gear lever, affectionately known as 'the porridge stirrer', was offered in later models as a neat remote gear change mechanism, which was more ergonomic in its location and allowed for quicker gear changing.

The Car Division made attempts to improve the aerodynamic efficiency still further by undertaking research to investigate the possibility of fitting an undertray to the engine compartment to improve airflow around the car. Research has identified that up to 20 per cent of drag in a closed car can be attributed to what is termed 'internal drag', which is the turbulence of the air flow through the engine compartment and its subsequent dispersal. However, the car company decided against any attempt to introduce such a modification on the grounds that it would reduce access for servicing the engine and components and the possible fire risk that could be caused by fuel collecting in the housing. If, however this modification had been possible the drag coefficient would have been even more impressive. In 1969 the Motor Industry Research Association undertook research to determine drag coefficients of 118 different cars. The 403 achieved fifth place. Considering that the test was more than twenty years after the design of the aerodynes, the results for the Bristol product from the 1969 testing was amazingly impressive.

4

Making the Car

The aircraft industry had exceptional safety and reliability factors built into every component and it was this outstanding approach to quality that would be transferred to the car production process. Hand formed coachwork using joinery standard wooden bucks were the order of the day for the body panels as already discussed in Chapter Three. Many other components were made in-house rather than buying in parts from elsewhere because they were regarded as inferior products. For example, front and rear suspension units were made in-house by the company whereas other manufacturers would buy in such units and accept the production standards of the manufacturer concerned. Door locks were made in house and according to Setright were almost burglar proof. In addition to the obvious aerodynamic efficiency of the new model there were many subtle changes to the construction which aided efficiency and durability inherited from aircraft industry expertise in working with aluminium. One change which dramatically aided durability of these models is in the grading of the panel thicknesses according to the function of each panel. For example, in areas where mechanics might rest their arms or weight, such as the car bonnet and upper surface of the front wings, a thicker 16-gauge alloy sheeting was used as against 18-gauge sheeting in other areas. Familiarity of working with aluminium allowed the company to generate a uniform panel hardness over the whole body which was achieved by the degree of panel-beating that took place on each panel. Aluminium has the characteristic that when it is being worked to shape by a panel beater it can harden during the process. This characteristic was used to advantage by using this technique in areas of the body of the car where extra strength was necessary. To undertake this method requires careful control by the panel beater and considerable skill to ensure the uniform hardness of the completed panel is maintained throughout. These noteworthy skills had been honed by the Bristol Aeroplane Company workforce during their vast experience of aircraft manufacture during the Second World War. Besides the number of components that were made in house, those that were bought in were subject to incredible scrutiny and quality control procedures. For example, carburettors were bought in, but were then dismantled and the components were lapped, or hand finished, to produce a perfect surface fit. This gave better performance and economy and, according to Setright, gave up to five mpg more per car. Quality control was such that high percentages of bought in components were rejected and returned to manufacturers who subsequently became more cautious when supplying Bristol Car Company with components.

This concentration on quality and mechanical efficiency was no more evident than in the production of the Bristol 2-litre engine. The original engine developed by the Bristol Car Division became the renowned sporting engine of its time and is still popular in historic car racing events today. Manufacturers such as Lotus, Cooper, ERA, Lister, AC, Tojeiro and Frazer Nash achieved much of their success due to the use of a Bristol 2-litre engine for their racing cars. The purity of the engineering and development is evident in the tremendous advance that was achieved in the power output from the original 85A engine of the Bristol 400. The variation was between 75 bhp and 85 bhp for the original type 400 car up to 150 bhp of the Le Mans specification engine. The latter had a compression ratio of 9.2 to 1. It was used in the type 450 Bristol racing car. Its impressive increase in engine performance was coupled with incredible examples of reliability even in racing conditions. This was ably demonstrated in the 1954 and 1955 24-hour Le Mans races. Three Bristol 450 racing cars were entered and came 1st, 2nd and 3rd in their class two years running. Long distance racing events were chosen to demonstrate the reliability of the Bristol engine. The success of the Bristol 450 was such that in both the 24-hour Le Mans races where Bristol

Cooper Bristol Racing car. (Mark Bishop)

Bristol 450 racing car. (BOHT)

Bristol 450 racing at Le Mans. (BOHT)

A later version of the 450 with an open top. (BOHT)

won their class, the racing team had the time and opportunity to arrange their cars coming over the finishing line in consecutive number order related to their racing numbers.

One sad outcome of the 1955 24-hour Le Mans race was the shocking accident involving one of the Mercedes-Benz team. The car, after collision with another competitor, was projected into the crowd of spectators opposite the pits. The result was many injuries, and eighty-three spectators were killed. The race was continued, which might seem surprising in the circumstances, but the logic of this decision was that if spectators all left the circuit at the same time this would delay the emergency services from reaching the victims to render assistance. It remains the worst ever accident at a car race to this day. On the plus side, it led to many safety improvements to racing circuits generally. Sir George White, the board of directors, and the racing team and employees were all profoundly affected by the tragedy. Subsequently the Car Division decided to withdraw from racing but donated all their prize money to the disaster fund for the victims and their families.

Following Le Mans, the Bristol 450 obtained success in the three-hour endurance trial at Montlhery and subsequently by a similar success in the six-hour speed records which were covered at over 115 mph. The car was then taken around the track at an average speed of 126 mph just to demonstrate that the engine was as healthy and oil-tight after the record-breaking attempt as it was when it started. For a small car company to achieve the success that they did in international racing and speed trials was enviable. Their success came from a dedication and obsession with quality and reliability in the engineering and design of their products. This experience was introduced into the upgrading and development of the production cars to the benefit of their customers. Much of the success of the Bristol engine must relate to the aircraft industry experience of the company and

Bristol engine racing cars coming in first, second and third in their class in consecutive order at Rheims in 1954. (BOHT with assistance of Michael Palmer)

the highly skilled workforce and inspectors, who brought aircraft quality standards to the production process. Jonathan Bradburn, who is part of a three-generation family car business who previously acted as agents for car sales stated in an article in Bristol Owner's Club Bulletin in 2022:

> I once took one sump apart for cleaning and noticed the material spec printed on the underside of the baffles, which indicated aircraft spec. I asked Eric Storey (a well-known Bristol Car Company Engineer) about this later as to whether they were using offcuts from the aircraft manufacture, to which he replied that they were not allowed to use anything that was not aircraft spec.

This was not only evident in the fact that the quality control and inspection routines were so rigorous, but that the assembly techniques and engine building were second to none. Engine combustion chambers were measured and calibrated to match perfectly, many moving parts of the engines were polished and balanced to achieve smooth running and reduce fatigue failures. This passion for perfection was expressed in the production of components such as the water pump impellor and the cooling fan. Both these items were statically and dynamically balanced with the cooling fan being a work of art. The fan blade was made in magnesium alloy to a true airscrew shape, which resulted in a most efficient blade. This was extremely light and yet durable. For warmer climates it was possible for the prospective owner to specify a four-blade cooling fan.

Above: Two-bladed airscrew-style
standard cooling fan. (Mark
Bishop)

Left: Four-bladed cooling fan
installed for owners living
in warmer climates. (Mark Bishop)

At the heart of the Bristol six-cylinder engine was the cylinder block cast in a chromium-iron alloy with the cylinder bores dry lined with brivadium austenetic steel, a material normally used in the aero engines made by Bristol Aeroplane Company. This material was renowned because it enabled Bristol aero engines to have a longer period of use before the necessity of overhaul meant that aircraft had to be grounded during this essential maintenance. The transfer of knowledge and best practice from one field of activity to another was a great success. It meant that many owners having only to renew piston rings after considerable mileages had been undertaken to revive engine efficiency. After considerable use of the engine, it was possible to rebore the existing liners rather than having to replace them. They could then be fitted with oversize pistons to restore performance. Another process adopted by the Car Division to ensure longevity and reliability of their engines was to use a nitriding steel of aircraft quality to reduce wear and this was used for the crankshafts and many other moving parts in the engine. There are many examples of engine rebuilds of very high mileage vehicles, where geometrical checks were unable to record any measurable wear on crankshafts. The existing crankshafts could be refitted following a light polish before reassembly. The light alloy cylinder head, which sat on the cast-iron block, was an unusual but efficient design with vertical and crosshead pushrods. This gave an inclined angle of 80 degrees for the overhead valves, only usually achieved by overhead camshaft engines. Despite this complicated valve operating system, according to Setright, the Bristol engine has been known to rev to 7,000 revs on a Cooper Bristol racing car. Such an incredible performance is probably not to be recommended as a rule. This tremendously successful engine has in recent years been subject to protests from elements of the historic racing community, who have suggested that historic cars with Bristol engines used in racing should be subject to a handicap. Unfortunately, this success has led to the demise of many road-going Bristol 2-litre models, which have been scavenged for their engines alone, leaving the remainder for scrap or to be fitted with a cheaper and less suitable engine type. Some of these alternative engines range from Jaguar and Triumph six-cylinder engines to even a diesel engine, giving various levels of sophistication as regards propulsion. To complement what was an outstanding performance for an engine at that time, the company undertook considerable research and development into the suspension and steering aspects of the cars. Independent transverse leaf-springs for the front suspension were used together with the company's own design of shock absorbers. The suspension system was protected by leather gaiters to prevent damage and ensure longevity. The combination of a live rear axle and torsion bars with the shock absorbers at the rear gave a combination of comfort and precise handling. The Bristol gearbox was subject to modifications over several years, but always retained free wheel in first gear. This feature enabled drivers to operate first gear without using the clutch. It was useful for drivers in slow-moving traffic as it enabled the driver to quickly select first gear without the jerky motion caused by the constant stop-start of traffic congestion. Early wheels used for the 400 were criticised as they showed a tendency to crack when under extreme pressure on the road or racetrack. The eight-gauge metal centres of the 400 wheels were increased to a four-gauge pressing later for the 401 to overcome this problem. The width of the wheels was increased by 12.5 mm at the same time. *Motor* magazine completed a 2,000-mile road test and indicated a genuine appreciation

A neglected 403 found in a barn which eventually formed the basis of a museum exhibit at Aerospace Bristol. (Geoff Kingston)

of the many qualities in relation to this aspect of the car with the following comment in May 1948: 'it clings tenaciously to the road when cornered fast on a dry surface' also 'a quite exceptional standard of comfort in riding over bad roads-exceptional by absolute standards.' (*Motor*, 19 May 1948)

5

Attention to Detail

Focussing on the detailed aspects of the design of the car demonstrates some important points about the quality of the design. An example of this is the quality of the finished paintwork. It is not surprising that the coachwork and paintwork were of a standard which was admired throughout the industry given the company's commitment to high quality. Each vehicle in preparation for the paintwork was hand finished by rubbing down the aluminium body to a state of accuracy of form. Without this attention to detail, the play of light on the completed painted body would be distorted and irregular. Making sure this was correct before any paintwork was applied secured a smooth and perfect finish. Many restored models in recent years fail to reach this standard, and the result is a ripple

An aerodyne being inspected during paint spraying operations. (BOHT)

Above: An inspector checking the paintwork to establish if the process of painting has revealed any irregularities in the panel beating. (BOHT)

Below: The play of light on the bodywork of a car that has no underlying irregularities in the final finishing of repairs to the aluminium skin will be in a straight line. The line will be irregular when finishing has been poorly executed. (Mark Bishop)

effect on the coachwork panels. It is said that up to sixteen coats of primer and finisher paint were used when preparing the coachwork. Each coat was hand flattened prior to the next application and subject to scrutiny at the works to ensure that it was up to standard. This approach to quality control won many accolades for the high standard achieved and resulted in prizes at national and international motor shows.

The brochure giving specifications for the details of cars itself reflects desire for sophistication throughout. It is understated and of simple design. Considering the small production numbers of cars, the company offered a wide range of colour schemes for exterior finish and internal trim. The immaculately finished external paintwork was available in eight standard colours: black, heather grey, Bristol red, lavender, surf blue, dark green, green metallichrome and Cambridge grey. This was a long way away from Henry Ford of Ford Motors in 1922 offering his customers 'any colour as long as it is black'. The high quality of the original paintwork has set a high standard for people restoring their cars today, but many have achieved these standards by following the company's example. In addition to alternative colour choices for the bodywork, upholstery colour variants included fawn, grey, red, brown, or blue. The interior trim was finished in top quality Connolly leather. Carpeting was offered in either brown or red, often with the edges trimmed in matching or contrasting colours. Wilton wool carpets were used throughout, even in the boot. The rear of the front seats was finished with cut moquette. Complete colour schemes were available to special order on request, which allowed for a degree of bespoke tailoring to meet customers preferences.

The headlights on the car are also worthy of note, as another indication of the quality of the vehicle. They are Lucas PF770 headlights and have a distinctive tri-bar format. This design of headlight was used by Rolls-Royce and Bentley and is a larger diameter than the standard headlights of car at that period and give a superior form of lighting. Fog lights were built into the front wings outboard of the main headlights and incorporated special yellow bulbs to aid driving in poor visibility. The rear light housing

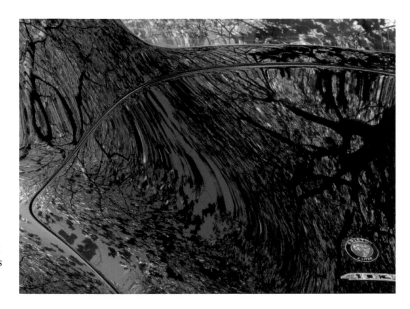

The paintwork on cars needs to be restored using the same standards that the original sprayers employed. (Simon Meeds)

In-house upholstery workshop at the height of production of the aerodynes. (BOHT)

performed three functions. It acted as a brake light, rear light and reversing light and this avoided the need for any extraneous additional lighting that would have marred the lines of the car and disturbed airflow. Semaphore trafficators were built neatly into the B-posts situated to the rear of the generously proportioned doors, in a housing at sufficient height to be noticeable. Their positioning avoided any projection that would have interfered with air flow and spoilt the purity of the line. The company had complete confidence that the vehicle would be capable of towing another vehicle if required as they provided holes in the overriders to facilitate the addition of a towing bar between the overriders. These overriders were attached over the integral bumper chrome strips as a means of protection to the bumper and were bolted through to the sprung steel bumper supports.

Above left: The high quality PF770 headlights as used by Rolls-Royce and Bentley have a distinctive tri-bar structure. (Mark Bishop)

Above right: Integrated fog lights. (Mark Bishop)

Semaphore indicators were cleverly housed to avoid unnecessary wind resistance. Positioning at height makes them easily visible. (Mark Bishop)

Front overriders provide good protection in the event of minor collision. (Mark Bishop)

Rear overrider with towing eye to accept a steel bar between the overriders to facilitate towing if required. (Author)

A comprehensive array of instruments was provided in a manner which often made people refer to the front of the control panel as 'the cockpit' and it is often likened to an aircraft instrument panel. Within this area the displays include rev counter, speedometer, oil temperature gauge, oil pressure gauge, water temperature gauge, fuel gauge, ammeter, and clock. Radios were one of the few optional extras. The lighting intensity for the instruments could be adjusted via a rheostat switch on the dashboard to avoid the distraction of excess light to the driver when driving at night. Above the windscreen two felt material roller sunblinds were located with a unique scissor action frame. This allowed the driver infinite adjustment over a wide range to suit the weather conditions. The rear window

Left: A close-up image of the speedo. The lettering is restrained and distinctive of the early 1950s. (Mark Bishop)

Below: The notable mahogany dashboard of a 403. (Mark Bishop)

Internal view of the infinitely adjustable sun blind. (Mark Bishop)

External view of the chromed scissor action mechanism of the sunblind. (Mark Bishop)

was provided with a blind that could be operated by the driver from his seat using an integrated wire cable. The driver could respond promptly to headlight glare caused by vehicles approaching from the rear or rear sun glare. It also had the effect of securing greater privacy for the occupants when required. The boot also received an automatic boot light that came on when the boot was opened via the pull knob from inside the car behind the rear seat central arm rest. This aided luggage removal or loading at night. All interior lights were designed in an art deco style and made of frosted glass. Housed under the dashboard was a brass foot pedal which controlled the Enots central chassis lubrication system. Owners of cars were advised to depress this pedal every 70–100 miles to adequately lubricate the king pins, track rod ends and feed the rack and pinion steering unit. This avoided the necessity for separate grease nipples, which is the traditional way of keeping these components lubricated. While the Enots system is not unique to the Car Division, it is an illustration of the attention to details that is characteristic of the company's work. It is a considerable convenience for the driver or as described by a leader writer in *Autocar* on 7 March 1952 as 'a boon to the owner and one that represents a substantial economy in the course of a year'. A rather basic Clayton heater was an option for the 401, but for the 403 a more sophisticated engine generated heating system was made available as a standard fitment. This incorporated two separate heater radiators and aircraft type grills or anemostats, which added to the impression of an aircraft cockpit.

In the quest for aerodynamic efficiency the engineers sought to avoid any external protuberances which would mar the clean lines of the body and in this respect, they were innovative with their solutions. The bumper design was integral with the bodywork both at the front and rear of the car, thereby reducing turbulence and improving the drag coefficient figure. No mascots or petrol filler caps protruded from the bodywork and even wing mirrors were excluded. Many owners, however, have violated the purity of the

Left: Air ventilation and heating grille in the aircraft style, which give even and quiet air distribution. (Mark Bishop)

Below: Integrated bumper to reduce interference with airflow and nevertheless protect the structure. (Mark Bishop)

design by attaching wing mirrors to the bodywork in the interests of road safety. One can appreciate this concern, but the author feels that a less invasive solution might be the use of overtaker door window mirrors, which safeguard the integrity of the design and can be easily removed without damage to the coachwork.

Another innovative feature to safeguard the integrity of the smoothness of the bodywork was the integral petrol filler cap flap, which was housed into the nearside rear wing and operated from a push button on the rear nearside passenger armrest. The push button

Added wing mirror on 403 can be removed without damaging the bodywork. This style minimises wind resistance. (Mark Bishop)

The line of the wing of the aerodynes incorporates the aperture for the petrol filling cap without affecting air flow. (Mark Bishop)

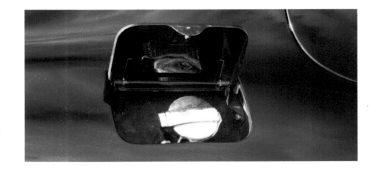

Access to the petrol filler cap is operated from inside the car by push button. (Mark Bishop)

system was also used to operate the driver and passenger doors enabling driver and passenger to unlatch the door at the first push. A second push would allow the doors to spring open fully. Once open the doors are retained in that position by an internal spring, which means that a person can emerge from the car without the door swinging closed and inhibiting their egress. The push button mechanism lies completely flush with the bodywork, which results in an uncluttered exterior appearance, but is also aerodynamically efficient as already mentioned. This system avoided any external protruding handles which would have affected airflow.

A similar internal system of operating methods was used for both the boot opening and the spare wheel tray access. The boot lid raises automatically when activated through a spring released operating arm. There is a surprising amount of space for luggage as befits a touring car. The capacious nature of the boot led to the story told by L. J. K. Setright, that when taking a car for a meeting Anthony Crook[4] would get a chauffeur to drive the car. He would hide himself in the boot, even though he was over 1.8 metres tall. On arrival at the meeting the chauffeur would release the boot and Crook would jump out unscathed in a smart three-piece suit. The boot capacity demonstrated by his stunt is of 4 cubic metres of luggage space, a very generous amount. Storing the spare wheel within the boot is a common solution to providing a spare in the event of punctures.

Model operating the internal push button door opening, which appeared in original publicity material. (BOHT)

Right: Model operating the internal boot opening – an image that appeared in original publicity material. (BOHT)

Below: The boot is revealed to show capacity for considerable volume of luggage. (BOHT)

This system was used for the early models of the 400, but it can result in inconvenience as the boot must be emptied to gain access to the spare wheel. The neat solution of storing the spare wheel below the boot compartment in the 401 design avoids this problem and yet keeps the spare wheel clean and secure. Luggage space is gained in the boot, and it is kept free from contamination from used road wheels in the event of a change of wheel being required.

The task of changing a wheel is aided by an inbuilt jacking point on each side of the car. This is situated in a position where the whole side of the car could be lifted from this single point to aid access. This is not only convenient but ensures a much safer situation for the mechanic or owner changing a wheel. The jacking point is welded to the chassis member and access for the geared mechanical jack is gained through an aperture between the outrigger and the chassis member. This aperture is neatly trimmed with a removable leather covered plate. At the bottom of the aperture is a rubber gasket cover to protect the structure from ingress of road dirt and moisture. The jack is stowed in a neat fixing in the engine compartment for easy access when required. The starting handle provided is similarly housed in the engine compartment with a series of clips that can be released for easy access.

Removing the spare wheel from the under tray. (BOHT)

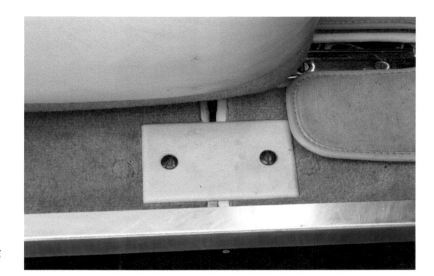

Aperture for access to jacking point. (BOHT)

403 jacked to show whole side of car raised from a single jacking point. (Mark Bishop)

Similar pull buttons also open the bonnet from inside the car. This can be done for either the right-hand side or the left-hand side of the car depending on which side of the engine needs to be inspected, a useful convenience for the driver or mechanic working on the engine. The bonnet can be removed in its entirety if needed and the self-aligning hinges facilitate replacement when work is completed. The result of the use of these mechanisms for opening the car, the boot, engine compartment, spare wheel and petrol filler cap is a particularly high level of security from theft for the owner. This secures luggage and other valuables and prevents the modern crime of syphoning off petrol. In addition, the internal storage in the vehicle was praised by no other than the renowned motoring journalist

Lawrence Pomeroy, who, writing in 1950 in his article about the 401 in *Motor* magazine, stated that: 'it will comfortably carry four people; in addition to them it will swallow an almost fabulous volume of luggage'.

With two lockable glove compartments, generous door pockets and the enormous boot capacity, together with the impressive performance, the future of the design as a GT car or Grand Tourer was assured. Furthermore, such was the integrity of the security features of the Bristol 403 car that the police described the cars as burglar proof. Indeed, the author had an experience to confirm this point on an occasion when he was locked out of his car at a local garage. The only way to gain access to the car was via the rear quarter light that was much too small for adults to enter. The garage owner, intent on helping to gain access to the car, selected a small child in a baby buggy passing by with his mother. The child was posted through the window and obeyed instructions to open the door.

The detailed consideration to every aspect of the design described is a particular characteristic of the cars. One remarkable aspect of the workforce is the long periods of service given by many employees. One anecdote in respect of this long service is that a visiting businessman asked the management team about the rates of staff turnover. The response was 'what turnover?' Syd Lovesy, for example, served for his whole career. Eventually he became Works Manager and did not retire until the company went into liquidation in 2011 when he was aged ninety-two. Many other employees were similarly loyal to the company, a considerable number serving over forty years. This continuity almost certainly contributed to the fact that employees were passionate about the product and cared enough to ensure that every detailed aspect was correctly executed.

6

The Automotive Industry
Response to the 401/402/403

To assist in the post-war export drive, when home sales were being restricted by high levels of sales tax on new vehicles, the company were willing to sell rolling chassis to various coachbuilders for completion with custom-built bodies. The connection with Carrozzeria Touring of Milan has been discussed earlier with Bristol Cars being keen to utilise the superleggera form of construction on their post-Bristol 400 model production. Although Bristol Cars did not proceed to fully utilise the Touring saloon designs for their aerodyne models, there was nevertheless an influence in the styling of the Touring cars to enable Bristol Cars to develop their 401/2/3 models in a way which captured some of the Italian flair. However, the original Touring examples were heavily modified to appeal to the traditional Bristol customer and in the process produced a much more successful design solution. Touring of Milan are believed to have built at least seven cars on Bristol provided chassis, some of which were sold to AFN Frazer Nash for resale to foreign customers only as exchange earners.

Many other coachbuilders at the time were attracted to producing their own concept of a Bristol based car, but with the coachbuilders' particular body style imposed on the Bristol rolling chassis. At the 1948 Geneva car show no less than four completed cars were displayed based on the Bristol 400 and 401 chassis and running gear. Two of the cars were by Touring Superleggera of Milan and one by Farina of Turin. The final car was made by Langenthal, a Swiss company that built cars using the Bristol 400 rolling chassis.

The first Bristol 401 chassis to have a purpose-built body by a Swiss coachbuilder, Fritz and Ernest Beutler of Thun, was in 1949. This was not an unattractive vehicle with flowing, but perhaps not such aerodynamic lines as the original Filton-built Bristol 402. Beutler built two more cars based on the Bristol 401 chassis and running gear, one of which was another saloon model which had rather more chrome and flamboyancy than the original Beutler and was very different from the understated design of the aerodynes. The third car was a drophead with a wide front grill and minimum bumpers but contained a vestige of the BMW ovals at the front. Ghia Aigle, who became a separate entity from the main Ghia factory of Turin in 1953, set themselves up as Ghia Aigle located at Aigle, south of Montreux. They displayed a Michelotti design based on a Bristol 401 chassis, but it was much criticised on aesthetic grounds due to a rather protuberant bonnet line, which projected over the bumpers.

It was not only foreign coachbuilders who took an interest in producing their own versions of Bristol cars by utilising a 401 rolling chassis. A Wolverhampton based dealership, Bradburn and Wedge, designed a full four-seater drophead with a more spacious body than the Bristol 402, especially as regards boot space, but perhaps not so elegant as the Bristol Hollywood special. Another British based dealership, University Motors of London, decided to build through their subsidiary, University Coachworks Ltd, a drophead coupe. Designed in 1948, this was based on a Bristol 401 rolling chassis. In their publicity material they described the car as 'the Bristol 2 Litre Foursome Drophead Coupe Model 401'. This rather quaint description no doubt relates to the rather cramped rear seats on the Bristol 402 drophead, which had some criticism from motoring journalists. The University Motors 401 Drophead was bodied in steel rather than the alloy panelling of the Bristol product which made it much heavier, and this would have affected performance. The car, however, was more attractive than some other attempts to build special bodied vehicles and was aimed at high income clientele with fitted luggage as standard and a counter-balanced hood for one person operation.

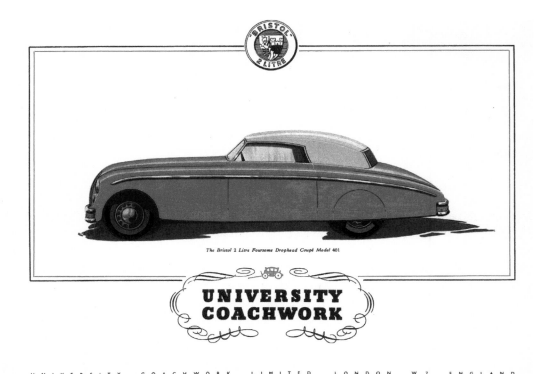

The Bristol 2 Litre Foursome Drophead Coupé Model 401

UNIVERSITY COACHWORK

UNIVERSITY COACHWORK LIMITED LONDON W 7 ENGLAND

Sales brochure image of the University Motors model – a derivative of the 401. (BOHT)

7

Public Reaction to the Car from its Original Introduction to the Present

The introduction of the new model, the 401, at the 1948 Earl's Court show was a great success and gave total credit to the amount of research and development that had gone on at Filton to produce the finished car. Motoring journalists gave the car high praise. Laurence Pomeroy, in 1950, stated: 'The particular merit of the 401 is a combination of virtues which may not be equalled in any other motorcar in the world.'

Many motoring journalists and other commentators from the arts have expressed their views in relation to Bristol car models generally, but the degree of positive feedback regarding the aerodyne models was exceptional. The functional qualities and the user satisfaction experienced have been well documented in test reports, with *Light Car* in December 1953 stating that: 'This is a car which is built with the sole purpose of providing the sporting driver with all the performance he wants – in luxury.'

A series of ongoing modifications during production of the 401 model continued. It included engine and suspension revisions, as well as alterations to braking mechanisms and a new gearbox. This continual refining of the specification to achieve the excellence that the Bristol Car Division aspired to eventually developed into the model Bristol 403, referred to by Oxley and other commentators as the 'definitive Bristol'.

The aerodynamic efficiency of the new model was amply demonstrated by the exploits of Anthony Crook, a well-known racing driver and Bristol car distributor who demonstrated the capabilities of the 401 at Montlhery racing circuit outside Paris. It was a popular sales promotional pitch at the time for motor manufacturers to claim that their new models could sustain a 100-mph average for an hour at the French circuit. The Riley car contingent were at the circuit attempting to demonstrate that their 2.5-litre saloon could achieve such a performance when Anthony Crook arrived in the new Bristol 401 model. Riley claimed that their car was faster than the Bristol model and that you could purchase three Rileys for the price of a Bristol. Anthony Crook had driven from London to Lympne Airport where he and the car were flown in a Bristol Freighter aircraft to Le Touquet, thereafter driving

Loading Tony Crook's 401 on to a Bristol Freighter on the way to speed trial at Montlhery. (BOHT)

on to the Paris Motor Show and then to the track at Montlhery. After a few circuits of the track to familiarise himself with the contours and camber of the surface Anthony Crook lapped from a standing start at 104 mph for an hour with a best lap at 107 mph. This was much to the chagrin of the Riley team, who were still struggling to reach the 100 mph in an hour with their 25 per cent larger engine than the Bristol.

The performance benefits of the new aerodyne body shape were evident in not just the example at Montlhery, but in many other competition events related to rallying and production car road races. During the time when the *Daily Express* newspaper sponsored a one-hour duration production saloon car race at the Silverstone circuit the aerodynes inevitably won their class and often the team prize. It was at one of these races that Anthony Crook, a Bristol enthusiast, who in 1973 became full owner and director of the Bristol Cars, beat the famous professional racing driver Roy Salvadori to win first place.

It is also interesting to note how members of the public react to the car currently. Drivers of Bristol 401 and 403s have noted that if anything reactions to the car are more extreme and enthusiastic now than hitherto. One driver commented that the 'wow' factor has increased with time, although the car's elegant appearance has remained constant. All drivers pointed out that people constantly wave and give thumbs up signs when they see the cars and have even been known to blow kisses or, on one memorable occasion, step into the road and kiss the bonnet while the car was waiting at traffic lights! A recent display of

Above: Tony Crook racing 401 at Silverstone. (BOHT)

Below: Fiona Bruce inspecting a Bristol 403 at the Antiques Road Show at Aerospace Bristol. (Author)

403 found with no engine or gear box, which formed the basis of the museum exhibit by Spencer Lane Jones on behalf of BOHT. (Geoff Kingston)

Bristol Cars and buses at the *Antiques Roadshow* at Aerospace Bristol evoked considerable public interest, including from Fiona Bruce, the presenter of the programme.[6]

More significantly, Bristol Owners' Heritage Trust, in collaboration with the Aerospace Bristol Museum at Filton that was opened in 2017, have provided an exhibit to explain the design of the aerodynes. The exhibit marks the formation of the Car Division of the Bristol Aeroplane Company as part of the long history of the aerospace industry in Bristol. It consists of a complete Bristol 403 that has had part of the body cut away to reveal the superleggerra construction. It enables the public to see the way that the car was made. According to museum staff, it represents the second most popular exhibit after the complete Concorde aircraft that is also housed in the museum.

In compiling this account of the aerodynes, it was felt that as well as noting public reaction to the cars it would be of interest to ask the owners of Bristol aerodynes about their opinions and experiences of driving an aerodyne. Approximately 10 per cent of existing owners responded. Most drivers feel that the cars are well suited to current driving conditions, particularly when provided with an overdrive and servo assisted disc brakes. This modification was included on the last six 403 cars by the Bristol Car Company. Most drivers had replaced the semaphore lights with more conventional indicators installed as part of the existing lighting, mainly for safety reasons. Some owners do feel that the cars are too precious to drive and tend to enjoy their cars in local settings on a limited basis,

Above: The museum exhibit under preparation in the Brabazon hanger. (Stefan Cembrowicz)

Below: A refurbished 403 cut away to enable the public to observe its structure and engineering details. (Photographed by Mark Bishop with permission from the museum Aerospace Bristol)

but many have used their cars for long periods of time as day-to-day transport. One owner commented that his local garage owner had recently checked the car for its MOT. After driving the car, he could not believe how well it drove on the road. He said that it was equal to any modern car and was amazed that the car was over sixty years old. Many drivers spoke of the sense of being at one with the car and noted the direct connection between the driver and the machine, a point that was enhanced by what was described as excellent ergonomics, so that whatever was needed was within easy reach and was completely comprehensible. The quality of the ride and precise handling were complimented by every driver consulted. It was often described as responsive, fast, and agile. Owners clearly appreciated the note of the engine and exhaust, although some described it as quiet, to others it was musical and only second to a V12 Ferrari. Members of the public also mention its distinctive sound. All owners regarded the design as iconic.

8

Justifying the Iconic Status

To justify the term design icon, which is the motive for this publication, it is necessary to have criteria against which the assertation can be judged. To this end it was decided to examine a set of design criteria from established sources to enable a comparative analysis to be undertaken to validate the claim that the Bristol 403 is a design icon. The first source examined was the *Ten Principles of Good Design* introduced by Dieter Rams in the late 1970s. Rams was a product designer who in 1957 developed a theory about what constituted good design. Whilst he was a furniture designer, the principles he established have been applied to many other products. These ten principles of good design will now be examined in relation to the ultimate aerodyne model the Bristol 403, in the conviction that this model can genuinely be esteemed as a design icon.

1. Good Design is Innovative

According to Rams:

> The possibilities for innovation are, not by any means, exhausted. Technological development is always offering new opportunities for innovative design. But innovative design always develops in tandem with innovative technology and can never be an end in itself.

A design might be said to be innovative if it breaks new ground or addresses established problems in a different or creative way. The innovation in the design process that produced the first of the aerodyne models came from Bristol Aeroplane Company's long experience as a maker of aeroplanes, buses, trams, and many other products, such as sailing dinghies and prefabricated houses. The wide range of products produced by the company gave them expertise in many different areas of production and the research and development challenges of these projects prepared them very well when they diversified into making cars. In relation to the development of the aerodyne models the use of the superleggera lightweight form of construction enabled advances to be made associated with improving power to weight ratios. This enabled the aerodyne models to have surprisingly impressive performance on the road, considering that the engine was of only 2 litres capacity and that the model was a four- to five-seater saloon. This performance is much greater than would normally be expected of a 2-litre engine. Jay Leno said that the 403 'is a two-litre car that thinks it's a three-litre car'. Leno became famous as the host of *The Tonight Show* in the USA and subsequently launched what became a prime-time television show called *Jay Leno's Garage* in 2015. The show is now available on YouTube and to say that Leno is enthusiastic about the 403 in this film is an understatement. In comparison a 2.5-litre Riley of the same era struggled to reach 100 mph when trials took place at Montlhery in 1950, despite having a larger engine capacity. The use of aluminium bodywork panels contributed to the power to weight ratios and thence the improved performance, but the major innovation was in the field of aerodynamics.

With their aeronautical experience Bristol cars were able to take advantage of wind tunnel testing facilities and produced suitable scale models to test in the wind tunnels at Filton. This development resulted in the Bristol 401 becoming the first wind tunnel tested production car. This innovative technology of a wind tunnel allowed Bristol Aeroplane Company's car division to modify the design to produce a product with very effective drag coefficient figures which again added to the excellent performance figures of the car.

2. Good Design Makes a Product Useful

According to Rams:

> A product is bought to be used. It has to satisfy certain criteria, not only functional, but also psychological and aesthetic. Good design emphasises the usefulness of a product whilst disregarding anything that could possibly detract from it.

Not only was the Bristol 403 regarded as a vehicle with a high degree of aesthetic appeal but psychologically was regarded as an exclusive quality car with considerable safety features which enabled Bristol Car Company at this time to claim that nobody had ever been killed in a Bristol. Safety features inherent in the design included a particularly strong chassis combined with the light but robust superleggera construction. Modern car design concentrates on avoiding accident damage to passengers and driver by providing crumple zones for possible impacts in the event of collision. These crumple zones included front and rear damage protection initially, but more recently have focussed on side impact in addition as pioneered by the Volvo company. Road accidents were a relative rarity in the 1950s because of the low rate of car ownership and the fact that heavy goods were mainly transported by rail. Nevertheless, the chassis and construction used in the manufacture of Bristol Cars meant that they stand up well to accident damage. It was perhaps for this reason that the Motor Research centre, as mentioned previously, used old Bristol cars for destruction testing in relation to their seat belt research. This was because it took three crashes to damage a Bristol aerodyne to the extent where it could not be used for a further crash test, whereas other vehicles only survived a single crash experience.

Another example of the strength of these models was the unfortunate crash of two competitors in the 1949 Alpine Rally, who ended up in a 60-metre-deep ravine after an accident. They both survived the incident, almost certainly because of the resilience and strength of the body structure. It is not unusual for motoring journalists to become lyrical after road testing the aerodynes as is perhaps illustrated by the comments of *Autosport* 1953 after their road test and several laps of Silverstone and Brands Hatch:

It was one of those journeys that live long in the memory, and whether you regard the Bristol as the most sybaritic of sports cars, or as a luxurious magic carpet with an incidental turn of speed, the result is such deluxe transport for five people and their luggage as one never thought that a car of only two litres could provide.

It is worth dwelling on whether the car has preserved its usefulness over time to consider whether it can be said to be useful now. There are several reasons why it could be argued that it has remained useful despite seventy-five years of car development that render some cars of that era no longer useful. It provides space for four or five people with adequate leg room for long journeys in considerable comfort. Whilst it does not have air conditioning that many modern cars are provided with, the arrangement of ventilation provides through draught to improve passenger comfort in hot conditions. This is achieved by the provision of vents that can be opened in hot weather and side rear quarter lights that facilitate a through draft to keep the car cooled by natural methods. In cold weather the heater works effectively, and the same vents distribute warm air throughout the interior. The ventilation system described also enables effective demisting of the windscreen and windows. Of course, seat belts were not available or known to be an effective means of alleviating accident damage to passengers at the time of manufacture, but a simple modification can easily enable seat belts to be fitted for extra passenger security and as indicated above the accident protection is surprisingly good considering year of manufacture. The design of seats in modern cars has received considerable attention to achieve lumbar support and headrests to reduce the chance of whiplash injuries. The seats in the 403, nevertheless, achieve a reasonable level of support for passengers and drivers and most people find the seating, particularly where it has been refurbished to address wear and tear, to be perfectly adequate. Boot storage, as discussed in chapter five, is commodious and more than adequate for long distance family touring. Two lockable glove compartments enable storage of valuable items out of sight. Side pockets in the doors are more than adequate for storing personal items.

Petrol consumption is a cause for considerable concern for many drivers particularly as prices at the time of writing have risen astronomically. The car cruising at 60 mph achieves between 24 and 26 mpg depending on specification but this can be improved to achieve up to 30 mpg with an overdrive fitted. This is deemed reasonable by most drivers and compares favourably to some cars of that era that achieve substantially lower figures. The generous petrol tank of 77 litres enables long distances to be covered before requiring further fuel. Motorists in some older cars are used to being castigated by the drivers of modern cars because they are travelling at low speeds. The Bristol 403 can keep up with modern traffic with no difficulty, another factor that demonstrates the usefulness of the car even after the passage of time. It is mentioned previously that the last six 403s manufactured were given some further updates such as front disc brakes with servo assistance and an overdrive that enabled motorway cruising. This demonstrates that the company continued to innovate and make adaptions to their models as opportunities arose. Many owners, including the author, have upgraded their brakes in line with Bristol Cars' modifications to improve braking and enhance safety. Experiments to provide an overdrive included alternative ways of achieving this, either through a factory modification or by alternative overdrive conversions by independent engineers.

The engineering quality of the car has facilitated its longevity and contributed to the fact that the car needs relatively limited amounts of maintenance and costly repair. Lubrication of the car through the simple depression of a pedal under the dashboard reduces service costs by oiling the suspension and steering rack. This is more fully described in chapter four. Compared to modern cars where electrical faults often outnumber mechanical and require specialist inputs or replacement parts, the electrical system on the car is very simple. It has only two fuses and three relays. Faults can easily be dealt with by an amateur. The original semaphore style trafficators have become rather outdated, and most owners have replaced these with flashing indicators as required by current regulations. This can be accommodated through the existing fog lights at the front of the car and through the existing rear lights with the use of LED lights, which give a brighter light and use less current.

3. Good Design is Aesthetic

According to Rams:

> The aesthetic quality of a product is integral to its usefulness because products we use every day affect our well-being. But only well-executed objects can be beautiful.

According to Keats' 1888 poem *Endymion*, 'A thing of beauty is a joy forever: its loveliness increases; it will never pass into nothingness'. Good design is something which never diminishes with time and is inherent in beautiful objects. This longevity of good design to permeate the senses and affect our personal satisfaction and well-being stems from the fact that only well executed objects can be beautiful. There is no doubt that the Bristol Aeroplane Company's products were well executed, the purity of the engineering and the extensive research and development which was carried out to produce the aerodyne models is documented here and in many other sources. To confirm the opinion on quality that is required to be accepted as good design the comments from a 1947 edition of the *Irish Times* states: 'One does not find good or serviceable machines at Bristol. There they only tolerate those that are perfect'. One guiding principle for design is the famous French architect Le Corbusier's declaration that 'form follows function', which was used throughout his international career as a designer of individual houses, churches, huge housing complexes and even complete towns. This idea that good design arises when an object's function leads the designer to a solution is endorsed in the statement from R. Pirsig in the worldwide bestselling book *Zen and the Art of Motorcycle Maintenance*. Using a journey with his son on a Honda 1966 Super Hawk across the USA, the author explores philosophical concepts, including what is the nature of quality. He goes on to give an in-depth consideration of its meaning and applies it to the motorcycle, but also to the individual's attitude towards technology and life itself. The principles can be applied to any product including a car. Pirsig states: 'What is Quality? Quality, for example, is not something you add like tinsel on a Christmas Tree; it is the cone from which the tree must start'.

The ethos of the Bristol Car Division in designing and manufacturing the aerodynes embodies this idea by allowing the purity of the engineering to shine through. There is no reliance on frills and furbelows to achieve the overall quality. The consensus regarding the final styling of the bodywork as regards its aesthetic appearance has always been very positive. Palmer in 2015 describes the sweeping lines of the aerodynamic body form together with the multi-curvature of the rear quarters, which give the cars the quality of 'artistic purity from any angle'. The aesthetic appreciation of car design has received numerous positive comments from motoring journalists and at least one renowned art critic. In 2006 Brian Sewell, art critic of the *Independent* newspaper wrote: 'the beauty of this essential rightness of design is even more startling in the rear .... To gaze on this Bristol from behind is to contemplate a work of infinite abstract, aesthetic, and sensual pleasure.'

Sewell first saw the Bristol 403 parked in Genoa against the textured surface of the wall of a palace and admired the contrast between the gleaming smoothness of the body of the car and the rough wall. He compared it to an abstract sculpture. This continued reverence of the ground-breaking design of the aerodyne series supports the concept of the model being a design icon reinforced by Brian Sewell's quote, which continued with the view that: 'The Bristol shell deserves to hang in the great galleries of modern art.' Once again it was the Bristol passion for quality and efficiency together with durability that led to the

Aesthetic exquisiteness of form. (Michael Palmer)

Above: Three aerodynes displayed at Kingsweston House in Bristol. (Mark Bishop)

Left: Rear view of a 403. (Andy Gibbs)

Rear view of a 403. (Mark Bishop)

eminence of the aerodyne models and the frequent comment that these models were the 'real Bristols'.

The Bristol aerodyne models, and in particular the 401 and 403 saloons, have been regarded as design icons with an intrinsic quality related to its aesthetic exquisiteness of form evident from the first appearance of the 401 model at the 1948 Earl's Court Motor Show. It is the overall design of the vehicles that generates the most significant responses from observers with both verbal and physical responses being drawn from onlookers. Positive responses to the design of the Bristols appears to have increased in recent years, perhaps because so many modern cars that have resulted from computer-aided design look very similar. The response to the styling of the cars was unusually referred to at length in the report in *Autocar* on 26 November 1948, which stated that 'the new car was possessed of that grace which comes of modern design'. Most motoring journalists tended to concentrate on the performance and engineering aspects of new models, concerned with top speeds, acceleration, roadholding and sometimes fuel consumption. Few gave accolades in relation to the external design quality. but as mentioned above the new Bristol models did elicit some favourable comments on this aspect of the vehicles. John Bolster, writing for *Autosport* on 28 August 1953, was relieved that the new Bristol 403 model retained 'the artistic purity of form' previously found in the

401 model. Bolster had previously tested the 401 model for *Autosport* on 1 August 1952 and was impressed by the 'well-bred purity of line that causes it to stand out in any company'. His experience of having had the opportunity to compare the 401 and 403 models in just under a year apart allowed for a comparative analysis of how the later model had developed in the intervening period. He stated:

> On relinquishing the 403 ... I recorded it as one of the few really great cars that I have handled, and which I would definitely buy for myself if I were in a position to do so. It is in fact much better than the already excellent 401 in every important respect and it is astonishing that so great an improvement could be achieved in such a short time.

Praise indeed from a renowned motoring journalist, writer, and racing driver. These comments confirm the progress in development which had occurred over such a limited period through improvements to the engine, gearbox, suspension, and braking system, which generated the conclusions of Bolster in relation to the Bristol 403.

4. Good Design Makes a Product Understandable

According to Rams:

> It clarifies the product's structure. Better still, it can make the product talk. At best it is self-explanatory.

The aerodyne Bristol car models have always generated a response, related to their appearance, which is axiomatic even when the observer knows little about the manufacturer or motor cars generally. This is because of the clear statement that the design makes in relation to being not just a thing of beauty, but an automobile of a distinctive character with obvious sporting potential. The result of its flowing lines and the streamlined shape, immediately communicates that it is a fast car with many comments such as 'it looks like it is doing 60 miles per hour when it is standing still'.

In building the car the designers were careful to consider the user's needs. The adjustable sunblinds prevent dazzle and the Bakelite control knobs are neatly labelled to facilitate identification and they are shaded by a cowl over the instrument panel to avoid reflection in the windscreen. Control knobs are of two different designs. The knobs with a serrated edge are operated by turning and they operate the rheostats. The smooth knobs are push-pull operated. It means that the driver can easily distinguish the function of the control knobs by feel. The seats were made to be adjustable on a series of rails to accommodate drivers of different heights. The rake of the seat back had four different positions adjusted by a cam on the seat back to enable the driver and passengers to gain a comfortable seating position and enable the driver to safely adjust his or her surrounding to comfortably reach pedals, have a good view of the road and have easy access to control knobs and gear stick. The steering wheel has three different settings to relate to seat adjustments and enables the achievement of a comfortable and ergonomically appropriate position. Similarly, the brake and clutch pedals can be adjusted on their spindle to accommodate the driver achieving

Two different designs of control knobs showing push pull operation on the left and the turning action on the right. (Mark Bishop)

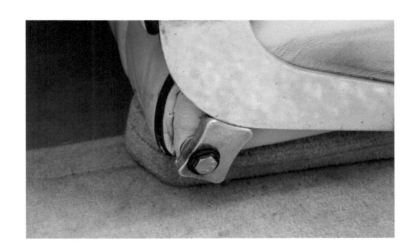

Seat adjustment for rake of seat. (Mark Bishop)

Runners for the forward and back adjustment of the seat. (Timothy Manley)

an ideal position. The provision of the Enots system of lubrication is also a great practical convenience for the motorist.

Laurence Pomeroy writing in 1950 for *Motor* reviewed the Bristol type 401 and stated: 'The particular merit of the 401 is a combination of virtues which may not be equalled in any other motorcar in the world'. He went on to say: 'Before moving a yard in the Bristol 401 it is clear that the men responsible for it are completely aware of the needs of the private motorist using this car for long-distance touring.'

5. Good Design is Unobtrusive

According to Rams:

> Products fulfilling a purpose are like tools. They are neither decorative objects nor works of art. Their design therefore should be neutral and restrained, to leave room for the user's self-expression.

It is not just the cognoscenti of the motoring world and the arts who can appreciate and understand the finesse of the aerodyne models, but the essence of the design concept is readily understood by people at large. This is because they can appreciate the sleek lines of the doors, bonnet, and boot panels together with the understated nature of the external trim. The push button door locks, which open the doors without external handles, and the integral bumper blades all contribute to what is described by Leno as: 'The most British of British cars, not flashy, mature and a well-crafted automobile'.

The lack of an excessive use of brightwork, such as insignia, mascots, obtrusive badges related to make, model and type are so discreet as to be hardly noticeable on the aerodyne models. The design of the wheels is unobtrusive and rather understated. The simplicity of the design contrasts very markedly with the design of the wheels of many modern cars, which seem to have been deliberately made ostentatious. Hub caps fit neatly over the wheel-nuts by a push fit over lugs welded to the steel wheels. The hub caps protect the wheel-nuts from damage and prevent the accumulation of road dirt around the wheel-nuts. The hub caps can be easily removed using a Bristol wheel brace provided with the car, which clips neatly into the tools section within the engine compartment. The perforations on the wheels form a pleasing pattern, but also fulfil an important function in allowing cool air flow over the brake drums. The medallions on hub caps and on the front and rear of the car are little larger than a fifty pence piece and have the Bristol City coat of arms and the words 'Bristol 2 litre' in tasteful script around the rim of the badge.

This discreetness led to an unfortunate incident when returning in our 403 from a classic car show in France where a French lady keen to read the name of the type of car she was following failed to stop at a roundabout, which we had stopped at because of traffic, and ran into us, much to her chagrin. She was very apologetic to have damaged 'votre belle voiture'.

Maybe more obvious model type badges might have averted the collision in this case, but on whole, the discreet brightwork and modest medallion badges are preferable. The boot and bonnet have a small 403 numeral badge, and the side panels have a discreet Pegasus coachwork emblem. This feature does not appear on a 401 and thus distinguishes the 403 model from the earlier 401.

Above: The design of
the wheels and badge is
simple and restrained
but distinctive.
(Andrew Gibbs)

Right: Coachwork
emblem of Pegasus, the
winged horse. (BOHT)

6. Good Design is Honest

According to Rams:

> It does not make a product more innovative, powerful or valuable than it really is.
> It does not attempt to manipulate the consumer with promises that cannot be kept.

The integrity of the design of the Bristol aerodyne models results in a product which provides the purchaser with everything required to enjoy the car to the full. *Automobile Topics* (August 1953), an American publication, states: 'It seems there are no "extras" to buy for the Bristol 403, since nearly every desirable accessory is fitted to the car at the factory.'

This was at a time when many car manufacturers only offered a spare wheel, heater and radios as expensive extras, which made the Bristol products appear very well equipped. The standard of equipment extended to the instruments, which were extremely comprehensive including oil temperature gauge, water temperature gauge, oil pressure gauge, petrol gauge, ammeter, and a clock. Naturally for such a sporting vehicle there was a rev counter and 120-mph speedometer. The honesty of the equipment indicated no intention to mislead potential purchasers with exaggerated instruments that might indicate higher performance than might be possible with the car provided. Although the 120-mph speedometer seemed generous for a vehicle road tested at up to 106 mph, many upgrades of the 2-litre Bristol engine were available, which would make the higher figure necessary to indicate speed. This was happening at a time when many manufacturers of what they regarded as sports cars had speedometers with very ambitious figures way beyond the Bristol example, sometimes up to 150 mph with little hope of achieving anything like such speeds.

Bristol Cars had a very low-key approach to the advertising of their cars with any adverts taken in the motoring press being of a discreet nature and somewhat understated They relied very much on their reputation and word of mouth referrals, a system which at times meant a waiting list for customers. The exclusiveness of the Bristols was such that at times some discretion was exercised by the sales team not to sell to certain individuals. It is said that when Anthony Crook sold cars from the Kensington High Street showroom, rumour has it that he locked the saleroom door if an unsuitable potential purchaser approached the saleroom. Such an incident is said to have happened to a well-known celebrity who Anthony Crook felt was not a suitable Bristol owner!

Many well-known people have owned Bristol cars, often coming from other expensive makes of car perhaps seeking the honesty, integrity, and reliability of the Bristol product. A well-known property developer, who having broken down on the way to an important meeting on the M1 in a luxury limousine of a renowned make, on being picked up by a taxi called to his chauffeur to get rid of the limousine and get a decent car. The chauffeur ordered a Bristol and the developer stayed with the marque for the rest of his working life with no regrets. One might ask why the developer's chauffeur chose to replace the existing expensive luxury car with a Bristol car. It seems that the chauffeur had many years of experience driving and maintaining luxury cars, such as Rolls-Royce, Bentley, Daimler and Aston Martin, as well as Bristol cars. It was his opinion that none compared with the Bristol for reliability. One aspect of reliability relates to the tendency for the half-shafts on some Rolls-Royce and Bentley models to break. A breakage would lead to immediate loss of traction and possibly the loss of the wheel in question, causing an alarming and costly breakdown. However, with Bristol engineering, broken half shafts were rare. According to L. J. K. Setright, if they happened, traction was maintained because the half shafts were designed so that the half shaft breaks in a section. In consequence, 'the ruptured surfaces tend to bind together and transmit tractive torque by stiction rather than by friction, while the hub construction keeps everything in engagement'. This engineering feature of the Bristol allowed gentle driving to be continued until it was possible to have the offending half shaft replaced. According to a Haynes publication of 1975 by David J. Voller, 'the Bristol 401/403 is regarded by many as one of the most beautiful British cars ever made.' Owning a Bristol car certainly attracted a range of well-known people including King Hussein of Jordan; Jimmy Carter, former President of the USA; Sir Richard Branson, entrepreneur; Peter Sellars, comedian and actor; Sir William Waldegrave, former MP; Noel Gallagher, pop star, and many others. It may have been reliability, handling, beauty or indeed the exclusive nature of a car designed in an understated fashion. To many of the purchasers cost of a car may not have been a strong factor in decision making but it is interesting to note that for a handmade product the cost was less than half of the price of a Bentley Continental, for example.

7. Good Design is Long Lasting

According to Rams:

> It avoids being fashionable and therefore never appears antiquated. Unlike fashionable design, it lasts many years- even in today's throwaway society.

The author has been asked by members of the public on various occasions about whether his 1953 Bristol 403 is a new car. Even though the design of the car dates back over seventy-five years from 1947, the simplicity and purity of the design spans the ages, and it still looks modern. It is difficult to establish how many of the originally manufactured Bristol aerodynes remain in regular uses. However, the Bristol Owners' Club register indicates approximately 170 known aerodynes amongst the membership. The Bristol Owners and Drivers Association[5], which has over 300 members, does not maintain a list of cars and of course some owners may not be members of either club. Seventy-five years on, this represents approximately 19 per cent of the number manufactured, which is quite an impressive figure that indicates the longevity of the vehicle given the small original production figures and the fact that many more may well be in existence, but unknown to the clubs. Driver Vehicle Licensing Agency statistics show a small but increasing number of registrations for the aerodyne models in recent years, which may be an indication that some owners are restoring vehicles that the club may have felt had been lost. This must be the product of the surge in value that has occurred in the classic car market, making it worthwhile to restore such vehicles. At a time when so many modern cars look very similar to one another, the individual style of Bristol cars generates an interest and demand which keeps the market buoyant.

The longevity of the design does not just relate to the innovative appearance of the product but must also have a quality which gives it durability that will not lead to an early discard of the object. This is where the Bristol cars have proved themselves time and time again. Many of the original vehicles are still in existence worldwide. Some are being used on a regular day-to-day basis as a single-family car. Even cars that have never been restored seem to continue to be used. One example known to the author appears regularly at car and tractor shows despite some degree of neglect. Others have been taken on extensive international touring trips, as far afield as North and South America, Australia and almost everywhere in Europe. In fact, the Australian branch of the Bristol Owner's Club, which consists of at least twenty-one members with Bristol cars, regularly undertakes trips of many thousands of miles. A striking example of a long-distance endurance rally undertaken in a Bristol 403 in recent years is the Peking to Paris rally. Paul Hickman and Sebastian Gross undertook this 13,695-kilometre journey in 2016 over a period of thirty-six days from the Great Wall near Beijing to the Place Vendome in Paris. In competition with 114 teams from all over the world, the pair achieved first place in class and eleventh place overall, an outstanding achievement in a car of that age.

There are many Bristol cars which were built up to seventy-five years ago that are still used regularly. This is due to the original design solution which used high quality materials and aircraft quality engineering. The massive 165 mm deep steel chassis and superleggera aluminium sheathed body, gave a longevity envied by many other motor manufacturers.

A well-used and unrestored 403. (Geoff Kingston)

A well-travelled 403 photographed in Mongolia competing in the 8,500-mile Paris–Peking rally in 2016. (Paul Hickman and Sebastian Gross photographed by Matt Watson)

8. Good Design is Thorough Down to the Last Detail

According to Rams:

> Nothing must be arbitrary or left to chance. Care and accuracy in the design process show respect towards the user.

The great advantage for Bristol Cars was that it was part of a large organisation, The Bristol Aeroplane Company, which had a long history of manufacturing aircraft since 1910, and therefore the quality of the product was to aircraft standards. One cannot afford to have quality control issues because, as they say in the aircraft industry, 'there is no hard shoulder at 38,000 ft'. This ingrained adherence to quality and quality control was followed in the car production plant, with many of the engineers involved in the building of the cars being previously skilled aircraft engineers. Although Bristol Cars built as many as possible of their car parts in house, the bought in products were subject to extreme scrutiny by the quality control staff at the factory. The degree of rejects on components supplied by various manufacturers were such that these manufacturers had to raise their standards to meet the stringent Bristol Car requirements. The attention to every detail of the car is more thoroughly explored in chapter five. It justifies the fact that the design passes the test to be regarded as thorough using Dieter Rams' criteria.

9. Good Design is Environmentally Friendly

According to Rams:

> Design makes an important contribution to the preservation of the environment. It conserves resources and minimises physical and visual pollution throughout the lifecycle of the product.

The long-lasting characteristic of the Bristol cars means that applying lifecycle costing merits the claim that Bristol cars are environmentally friendly. Critics may take the view that driving older cars with little or no control of emissions is environmentally irresponsible. This common viewpoint fails to consider other environmental consequences. For example, the number of replacement vehicles that one may have had during a fifty-year-plus lifecycle of a Bristol car is pertinent. Modern cars are designed for a short lifespan. After five to seven years or 150,000 miles most car dealers are not interested in the vehicle and many people replace their cars every five years. On this basis it could be assumed that up to ten replacement cars may have been built during the seventy-year lifespan of a car produced in 1953. The resources required to produce that number of replacement cars during that period would be considerable, but the environmental costs of disposal of more modern vehicles also needs to be considered. Current production methods include many non-recyclable elements such as plastics and electrical components. The Bristol benefits on this front by using a high level of recyclable materials such as steel, aluminium, wood, and glass. Very few plastic items are utilised other than the Bakelite control knobs. All the interior trim uses natural materials such as wool for the carpets, leather for the seats and internal door panels, and wood for the dashboard. The polluting elements of running older petrol-driven cars should also be considered against the point that because the engines are petrol driven, in the future it should be possible to run the engines on hydrogen fuel with no exhaust pollution. This could result in continued use in the future, thereby saving purchase of alternative replacement vehicles with all the use of resources that that would entail.

10. Good Design is as Little as Possible

According to Rams:

> Less but better – because it concentrates on the essential aspects, and the products are not burdened with non-essentials. Back to purity, back to simplicity.

Ludwig Mies van der Rohe (1886–1969), a famous international architect and furniture designer, was well known for his statement 'less is more', although the idea of simplicity and clarity in art goes even further back to a poem by Robert Browning in 1855. Whilst van der Rohe was mainly referring to buildings when he made this statement, the idea expressed has become something of a core belief for design communities. 'Less is more' expresses an understandable reaction to the decorative designs of the preceding Victorian period in many areas of design activity, not just motor cars, and in essence sums up the idea that a new age of modernism was emerging. Wartime experiences probably compounded the view that any design is better if simplified to its basic elements and not overdone. This idea is very much in the vein of another famous architect, Le Corbusier, who claimed that 'form follows function'. Both these maxims are embodied in the design solution of the aerodyne models with their unobtrusive form and purity of line and the inclusion only of features that contributed to functionality. In consequence, every aspect of the car has a function with no frippery or useless extras or additions to confuse the user. The simplicity and smoothness of the body shape is a result of the wind tunnel testing, which modified the original design concept to achieve the design icon that we have today. There is no question of perceiving this design as anything other than a post-war modernist solution. In fact, the view that might be taken here is that the car design was an early example of the minimalist style that has dominated the twentieth century and continues to be very influential to this day. Many people who selected Bristol cars, as mentioned, did so because of their unobtrusive designs.

Conclusion

Mention has already been made of the variety of positive responses that the aerodyne design elicits from people, especially when it is their first encounter with this example of the marque. The emotion shown by enthusiastic observers has been referred to earlier, with some more dramatic than others, such as the kissing of the bonnet by two mature gentlemen when held up in heavy traffic. A recent encounter involved overwhelming delight when a cancer patient passed by the car and exclaimed tearfully that seeing such a beautiful object had really made her day. This degree of response to an object that is seen as a thing of beauty has been said to be generated by arousal of the emotions evoked by the degree of perfection in the execution of the work. Albert Le Coff, Philadelphia, 2003, stated: 'When a work of art arouses emotion that is felt by everybody, its proportions are close to the golden section.' In making this comment Le Coff was contributing to the body of knowledge and understanding about what makes some man-made objects infinitely more pleasing than others. The answer according to many commentators is the proportions of the golden section. The golden section is not a measure, but a ratio of two homogenous dimensions. It is sometimes referred to as the divine ratio because the harmonious proportions are found in nature as well as man-made objects and even in the human body. The golden section is in effect an arithmetical ratio. Its use as a guiding principle can be traced back to the time of the pharaohs in ancient Egypt and the building of the pyramids. The proportions were also known to the ancient Greeks, who built their temples using this relationship and Vitruvius's canon of proportion. The medieval builders of great cathedrals, many of which evoke emotional responses and a sense of awe, are also examples of the golden section in operation. The relationship to the human body made famous by Leonardo DaVinci's drawing of a man inscribed in a circle and a square also demonstrates the golden section.

More recently Georgian architecture, influenced by the ancients, used the same proportions, and was also found to be a method that resulted in pleasing architecture. The Georgian terraces of historic cities such as Bath and Bristol are fine examples of this and many objects of art, when analysed, also reveal the golden section proportions. Interestingly many everyday objects, including modern day sports pitches, are all close to the golden section in that their length-width relationship complies. This would seem to indicate that the divine proportions of the golden section ratio have a functional element in addition to the beauty and harmony that is generated by their incorporation into a product design. The designer of any object may knowingly use the proportions of the golden section or in seeking to create both a functional and beautiful object may chance upon these proportions unwittingly. Buckminster Fuller, engineer and architect, well known as the designer of the geodesic dome, stated:

> When I'm working on a problem, I never think about beauty. I think only how to solve the problem. But when I have finished, if the solution is not beautiful, I know it is wrong.

Perhaps this sentiment expressed by Fuller was a designing principle for Bristol Cars. Considering the degree of enthusiastic and emotional response that have been generated during the author's fifty years of ownership of a 403, the possible connection of the link that there may be some intrinsic feature about the car that caused such responses. During research to assess the aesthetic considerations of the design of the car and to determine why it is considered by many people as a beautiful object, the golden section literature is pertinent. When applying the formula AC/AB =1.618 the proportions of the aerodynes fit with the golden section criteria.

This seems to explain why these cars are design icons as this benign proportion creates an object that is pleasing to the senses as well as functionally close to perfection in its performance.

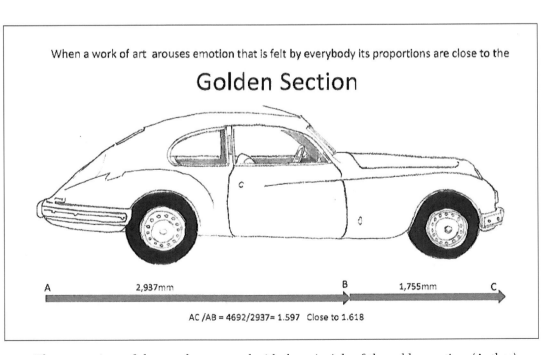

The proportions of the aerodynes accord with the principle of the golden section. (Author)

Drawing of a 403. (BOHT)

Buyer's Guide

If you have been enthused by this publication and want to consider joining the Bristol Car fraternity, below are a few hints and tips before purchase which may be of assistance and safeguard you from disappointment. Sources for information on cars for sale are the two owners' clubs, BOC and BODA, details of which are given in the Notes. Specialist Bristol car dealers may also be helpful. Wherever you might search remember that as Bristols are constructed on a substantial separate chassis and have aluminium bodies the likelihood of a Bristol being beyond repair is remote. Repairs and restoration however can be expensive depending on how much work one is able to do oneself or if everything has to be undertaken professionally. For this reason, it is best to acquire the best example possible and thereby have the joys of Bristol motoring from the word go. Here are some key points to consider:

Buy the best example that you can afford. Have the vehicle professionally assessed to enable any works required to be scheduled into your budget.

The engine, gearbox and rear axle are robust and last well if properly maintained. Oil changes at the recommended intervals are essential for longevity. Check for service records, MOTs and repair and or accident history.

The steel chassis tends to corrode where it extends over the rear axle, but the remainder of the chassis can be repaired more easily.

Check drain holes in doors, below windscreen, rear quarter light cills, as sometimes these have been welded up to stop corrosion of rear wheel arches. These drain holes are connected to rubber hoses to drain rainwater away from these components, so it is important that they are still connected and draining effectively. If not connected or blocked further investigation is recommended to check for corrosion.

Inspect bodywork for blisters which can indicate reaction between the alloy panelling and the steel supports where the factory fitted insulation has broken down. Early 401 models had issues with the bumper units corroding, but this was rectified in later versions and all the 403 models.

The interior trim is of very high quality and many aerodynes still have their original leather trim where it has been well nourished and maintained. The roof lining, if damaged, can be replaced, but the original material is almost impossible to obtain.

Instruments can be repaired if needed and new electrical looms are available if required. LED bulbs are available for most existing bulbs and give improved lighting standards and take less power to operate.

The Bristol suspension units are predominantly used as pivots and providing they are kept topped up are unlikely to need attention. The telescopic shock absorbers are readily available and produced by several manufacturers when replacement is required. Ensure that the Enots lubrication system is working and has been used as this keeps the front suspension safe from premature wear as well as the steering rack.

Useful upgrades for modern motoring conditions include:

Alternator and conversion to negative earth.

Overdrive-Common upgrade for Bristol owners

Front disc brakes with servo

Two-speed wiper motor

123 Electronic ignition

Anti-Ethanol petrol pump kit and carburettor gaskets

Stainless steel straps for petrol tank

LED flasher bulbs housed in rear lamp housing and front fog lights, can also adapt to become hazard lights.

In conclusion, Bristol cars are basically quite simple and straightforward to maintain and if well maintained will give hundreds of thousands of trouble-free miles of delightful motoring.

Postscript

It was with great sadness that the Bristol Car Company announced in 2011 that it was going into receivership. Many reasons have been given for the demise of the original car company and some may say that it was the development of the Bristol Fighter supercar that brought Bristol to its knees. The two-seater car had an 8-litre V10 engine with the S version producing 660 bhp and having a top speed of 240 mph. The aerodynamics were again an important part of the design and development process, and the Fighter had a drag coefficient of 0.27cd and could achieve a 0–60 time of 3.5 seconds. Despite this amazing performance and modern styling, the new car failed to rescue the ailing company finances.

The company was purchased by Kamkorp through its subsidiary Frazer Nash Research with a proposal to produce new models using advanced technology. Unfortunately, this has resulted in only one prototype example of a two-seater car with many bought in components and little else in the way of taking the company forward. The new company is in the hands of the liquidators and complicated lawsuits are ongoing to establish intellectual property relating to Bristol Cars Ltd.

Several interested parties are hovering in the hope of obtaining the rights to use the Bristol name and possibly reproduce some of the original Bristol models with updated specifications. Perhaps the Bristol name will be revived yet again, but hopefully with more success and reflecting the original calibre of the marque.

The Bristol Fighter supercar publicity shot. (BOHT)

Bibliography and Notes

Autocar No. 1343 (9 January 1948).

Balfour, Christopher, *Bristol Cars A Very British Story* (Sparkford: Haynes Publishing, 2009).

Bradburn, Jonathan, A Bristol Agent's Tale (Bulletin *173*, Bristol Owners' Club, 2022).

Keats, John, Extract from 'Endymion', poem first published in 1818, By Taylor and Hessey, London.

Oxley, Charles, *The Quiet Survivor* (Ramsey, Isle of Man: Oxley-Sidey Publications, 1988).

Palmer, Michael, *Bristol Cars Model by Model* (Ramsbury, Marlborough, Wiltshire, The Crowood Press, 2015).

Pomeroy, Lawrence, Account Rendered 1950.

Ford, Henry (in collaboration with Samual Crowther), *My Life and Work* (Doubleday Page and Company, 1922).

Setright, L. J. K., *Bristol Cars and Engines* (Motor Racing Publications, 1974).

Setright, L. J. K., *A Private Car: an account of the Bristol, The Word* (Palawan Press Ltd, 1998).

Notes

1. Bristol Owners' Heritage Trust is an organisation set up by BOC, whose main purpose is to preserve and conserve the history of the marque. bristolownersheritagetrust. wordpress.com
2. Bristol Owners' Club (BOC) has approximately 1,000 members and is the longest standing membership organisation for Bristol Car owners and enthusiasts. The club organises events and an annual concours.boc.net
3. L. J. K. Setright was a well-known journalist and writer. He wrote for *Car* magazine for over thirty years and wrote several books on cars and automotive engineering as well as contributing to many other publications. He was widely recognised as a knowledgeable engineer and an authority on Bristol Cars.
4. Anthony Crook was a racing driver and distributor for Bristol Cars. In 1960 he became part owner of Bristol Cars before taking full ownership in 1973.
5. Bristol Owners and Drivers Association are a membership organisation whose main interest is keeping Bristol cars on the road. Website: bristoloda.org
6. Aerospace Bristol is a museum of flight situated at Filton in Bristol. It includes the last Concorde to fly. An exhibit at the museum explains the contribution made by the Car Division of Bristol Aeroplane Company to industry in the city.